W0007612

RUMOURS: A MEMOIR OF A BRITISH POW IN WWII

BY CHAS MAYHEAD

A PLEASURE BOAT STUDIO BOOK

Mayhead, Chas

    Rumours : a memoir of a British POW in WWII / by Chas Mayhead. -- 1 st ed.

    p. cm.

    ISBN 1-929355-06-8

    1. Mayhead, Chas. 2. World War, 1939-1945--Prisoners and prisons, German. 3. World War, 1939-1945--Personal narratives, British. 4. Prisoners of war--Great Britain --Biography. 5. Prisoners of War--Germany--Biography. 6. Prisoners of war--Italy--Biography. 7. Prisoners of war--North Africa--Biography. I. Titles

D805.G3M39 202   940.54'7243

                                  QB102-702001

Design and composition by
Sharon Lee Ryder

For Roy Smart

Published by Pleasure Boat Studio: A Literary Press
201 West 89th Street, #6F
New York, NY 10024-1848
Tel/Fax: 888-810-5308
Email: pleasboat@nyc.rr.com
URL: http://www.pbstudio.com

Rumours: A Memoir of a British POW in WWII

By Chas Mayhead

RUMOURS:
A MEMOIR OF A BRITISH POW IN WWII
CHAS MAYHEAD

A PLEASURE BOAT STUDIO BOOK

SOMEONE SAYS, "I hear there's a train coming in with food supplies."
And immediately there's electricity. Wow. A train. A train! It was
never true, ever, not once while I was there, but it kept you going. Or
you'd hear there was an air raid, that the Americans or the British or
someone got through. Every day you'd hear something like that.
Hopeful news. None of it was true. You believed it, though, because
you needed to. Prison camp life was all rumours. Constantly. You lived
on rumours. Especially food rumours.

PUBLISHER'S NOTE: We chose to maintain the British spelling of
rumours in order to preserve the fact of the author's nationality, which
plays a major role in this book.

THE DESERT

WE THOUGHT WE'D MADE IT. Dawn had crept in and finally we could see the desert, what there was of it to see. Mostly hillocks of sand colored rosy and golden from the sunrise and shaded by the passing night, occasional clumps of vegetation off toward the horizon. We pulled off the road onto a knoll capped by a few scrub trees, climbed into the open back of the lorry, and downed a biscuit or two. We took turns keeping awake since of course we couldn't travel during the day. German aircraft flew overhead, but if they spotted us, they must have thought we were Germans. I suggested we stay put until it got good and dark again. The others agreed.

That evening, we drove away in the direction we thought was right. I was at the wheel. At around one or two o'clock in the morning, I saw something in the distance I could barely make out—a mass of black silhouettes dead ahead. It appeared to be a military camp but I couldn't be certain at that distance. On the other hand, we were too close to them to turn away—that would have been a giveaway. Still, I was afraid they were Germans. I woke the others and told them what was up. I thought we should take our chances and keep going. I didn't think we really had much of a choice. The others agreed, and we went on, very nervously. I'm surprised I could even keep the lorry going in a straight line. It didn't take long to discover that our fears had been realized: They were Germans, a Panzer group. Tanks. I don't know how many tanks there were, but there must have been more than a hundred, all lined up and spread across the desert. There was one main pathway down the middle. We headed for it.

We knew we were in trouble, but on we went. What choice did we have? It was dark as ink, so we thought we just might make it. We inched our way right down that pathway. A guard or two stood near every few tanks, but no one called out to us. We'd taken our hats off, of course, and our tropical gear didn't look much different from the German gear, so they obviously thought we were Germans. The lorry was pretty much nondescript, particularly in this darkness. Nobody among us was to speak no matter what happened. That was the rule. Nobody. Act like you're asleep. I drove very slowly, as though we were tiptoeing along in an attempt to be as quiet as possible. I was so scared I could taste steel deep in my throat. My mouth was dry but my brow was wet with perspiration. We could see the silhouettes of the German soldiers sleeping and occasionally we could see the guards. They didn't expect us to be British, of course. What kind of crazy British soldier would drive right down through the middle of a battalion of tanks?

I don't know how many guards we passed, but I knew one of them would say something. I had decided to say nothing if they spoke to me or else they would have known in a second that I wasn't German. I tried to act as though I was dead beat and just going forward by momentum. Some of them waved, sort of half waves. I waved back, shook my head, and moaned very softly, acting as though I was just going through the motions, trying to stay awake. That's all. But it seemed to work. I told myself we couldn't win; before long someone will say something and we won't be able to answer. But it didn't happen. Unbelievable.

We got to the end of the line. It was probably fifteen minutes, but I swear it seemed like an hour or more. It was near 4:00 a.m. by then, and we just kept going. None of us could believe we'd made it through. After we were out of sight, I finally stopped and said to the others, "We've made it. And by god, if we made it through that line, we can go anywhere!" We felt terrifically relieved. Of course we wondered why those tanks were all stationed there, so close together, and we knew something big was going on. But at least we'd made it through. I got in the back of the lorry to relax and let someone else do the driving for a while. I just wanted to get to our company and tell about the tanks we'd seen.

An hour or two later, with dawn approaching fast, we started talking about finding some cover for the day. Suddenly—*Pop! Pop! Pop!*—machine-gun fire. Someone was shooting at us! We got out of the lorry immediately, scrambling out like someone had just dropped a bomb in the truck. But then we were in the open with nowhere to hide and, to make matters worse, we didn't know where the gunshots were coming from. I tried to tell myself it might be the British firing at us, might be our own men who hadn't been able to identify us. But I didn't really believe it. We squeezed under the vehicle to escape the shooting, but that didn't really work very well. We then made a run towards a dry river bed and got down low. We were like rats forced to scatter from their nest.

In no time at all, voices in English called out to us: "Tommy! Hey, Tommy!" This was a reference to "Tommy Atkins," a name used for the English soldiers in WW1. It hadn't been used in this war, though, and we knew these were Germans.

Prologue
BEFORE THE WAR

W E ALL KNEW THERE WAS SOMETHING GOING ON IN E UROPE, especially in Germany, at that time, and of course rumours abounded regarding an imminent war, but I had seen in England the antics of Oswald Moseley, leader of the British Union of Fascists, and the men around him with their marching and saluting, so I didn't pay much attention to it all. I suppose I thought Germany wouldn't go into another war after their defeat in 1918. It seemed crazy. But I didn't realize at the time that Hitler was a madman.

Nobody believed in the possibility of war. In fact, Neville Chamberlain, our prime minister, told the country there was no problem, it would all be straightened out. He traveled to see Hitler in order to avoid a war, and he came back and said, "I have it here, the word of Adolf Hitler: No war." And we were all pleased about that because nobody wanted to see another war. Chamberlain managed to avoid war for a year, but it became ridiculous. Hitler and his entourage were monsters.

I was living at home at that time and earning only a small wage. That's the way it was. I was an office boy sitting on a stool and told to write "thick and thin" in a ledger of sorts, an old pen-and-inkwell job. I felt like something from a Charles Dickens story. About as well off, too! Well, the money I earned was paid to me on Friday, and I gave it to Mum right away; then she gave me a small amount back. Still, I managed to pay my own expenses, put some small amount away, and pay for an occasional big evening at the local cinema (the price being sixpence with a bar of nougat for one penny). I looked forward to that, an evening with the lads and girls.

It wasn't a bad life. Where I lived everyone seemed to share the same lifestyle, all in rented property known as "The Buildings," well known, actually. Nobody could afford to buy a flat or a house. That was a dream. I couldn't see myself getting away from where I was, breaking out, much as I wanted to. The future looked hard. Still there were few real complaints from my friends and neighbors. We all got on with life. I ate at home, Dad worked hard, and the rent was less than a pound a week, eighteen shillings six pence, that is. And the cigarettes were ten for six pence. We got by.

The Suit

Not far from where I grew up—at the Elephant and Castle District in London—stood a tailor shop called Levy's. It was really a modern tailor shop, even had hand-sewn lapels. You could easily see their suits were well done. That was the real thing to us: a well-made suit. We'd grown up old-fashioned, and I was expected to wear clothes like my father wore. But I wanted to be like one of the boys, not old-fashioned. I wanted one of those modern suits, stylish and up-to-date. And this particular tailor shop was so good, in fact, that they once had Max Baer come by just to be photographed in one of their suits. Max Baer. He was the heavyweight champion of the world. He happened to be in town to fight a bout, and Levy's invited him to come in. And he did it, too. Of course he was a handsome, well-built man, and I'm sure he sold a lot of suits for that shop. I saw him standing outside the shop in the suit they'd fixed for him and I've got to say that alone was an inspiration to buy a suit there.

I often saw well-known people, movie people, around London in those days, in the early thirties, people like John Wayne and Frederick March and Stewart Granger. I was a lad who liked to spot things which I knew weren't really so important, but I was just interested. I used to go autograph hunting. I liked the idea. I was always aware that I was living a fairly hard life and had very little money. But although that didn't seem to bother many people around me, it always bothered me. Not because I was ashamed. I figured I was as good as anyone else. But I wanted my life to be better than it was, that's all. Perhaps most of the fellows my age were thinking like me. I don't know. Maybe. But I knew what I wanted. I wanted to make some money, wanted to buy a home in the suburbs for Mum and Dad and to give them holidays. That was my dream. And I wanted to own a good suit.

Because of the times I'd walked past this shop, I knew he had the cut that was right for me. So I started to put money aside to buy a suit "on the never-never," as we used to say—so much a week.

I didn't want my suit just so I could be seen, though. My friend Bill Nash was making more money than I was, and he had two suits. He liked to be seen, and I felt a bit envious of him. I just wanted a nice suit, a really well-made suit that would make me feel good. You can't beat that. And you can't beat a fitting for a tailor-made suit. Fittings. I'd never had a fitting in my life. This suit would cost me ten shillings more than I'd usually pay, which would have been around two pounds fifty, or eighty bob, as we liked to say. I didn't care. So I went to this shop and I got the kind of attention they'd give to a celebrity. That's what I liked about it. They selected the material and laid it out. They asked me to feel it. What did I know? "Was it any good?" they asked. Sure it was. Of course. They told me what they would do, how the cut would be and how the stripes would come this certain way, and I said, "You've sold me. I'll have the suit."

"Yessir," the man said. "Very smart."

We agreed on a purchase deal, and, a bit embarrassed, I was measured for the suit. It would cost me three guineas and I loved it. This was living, really living. I felt like *I* was Max Baer. All I could think about coming home was how long it would take until I would get the suit.

I went back in a week and the tailor smiled and said, "Don't worry, you'll get your suit." He said he'd like me in for another fitting. I said, "Why? Was it wrong?" And he said, "No, but this is what we do." He told me it'll be half finished and they'll try it on me and see how it fits. And I thought, I'm living. This is what it's like to live.

I never told a soul. I never said anything to anyone at home. I went back to the shop for a second fitting. Sleeve, arm, "four buttons or three?" "Four!" I was getting a suit that was good enough for anybody in the West End of London. Anybody. It was about a month, but it seemed twice that, before it was ready. I went up there to get it and paid what they asked for. That suit was everything I could have expected. The quality was there, the fit was there. It was perfect. It was navy blue. And it had a small design in it. I knew what I was doing.

I took it home with a hanger they supplied that was bent so the suit wouldn't be damaged. The hanger had the firm's name inside. I still have that hanger. And I almost didn't want to put the suit on. I knew that anybody who wore this suit would be looking good. On Sunday I went out in it for the first time. I'd bought a James Cagney hat, or what I thought was a James Cagney hat. This was the thirties, remember, and Cagney was big. I pulled the brim down right over my eyes. The suit hung nicely. Not too tight. Just right. I wondered if Maggie, the girl down the street, would notice me now.

When I first came out in my suit, though, Dad never said a word. My sister told me it looked lovely. My brother didn't say anything either, and I think he was jealous. He probably had it in mind that he'd end up wearing it someday. (He did, too.) Those were days when you had good friends who would say, "I've got a date this evening and you haven't. Would you lend me your suit?" "Well," you'd tell him, "watch what you do with it when you're having fun and games and perhaps getting your trousers off." The suit was important to me. I was eighteen. Nearly a man, I suppose.

One reason I'm telling this little snippet on the suit is I remember when, in 1944, I was a prisoner-of-war in Germany and I received a letter from my brother telling me he was wearing my suit. It was his idea of comedy, I suppose, like he was trying to cheer me up. He said he wore it to take it out "for an airing." I've got to confess it upset me, but he couldn't have realized what that double-breasted meant to me. It's enough to be angry out there, and I guessed it would be cleaned and pressed for my return home.

Signing up

I had purchased a bicycle for three pounds when I was about sixteen, back in 1938, and I often used to ride out to the parks in Dulwich and Clapham, sit on the grass and read a magazine. I began to look around more and wonder what I could do to improve my future and to possibly, someday, afford some higher standard of life. Maybe even buy or rent a good home in the suburbs for my own family, with a car and a real garden. Then I could go and fetch Mum and Dad and give them some of the good times they deserved. Dreaming in the park.

One morning in the spring of that year my good friend John Haysen and I had planned to go to see a football game together, but at the last minute he came by to tell me he'd made a date with a girl and wouldn't be going with me. I wasn't overly pleased about this because I used to look forward to those once-a-week outings. It hurt and I guess I was envious, but I decided to take a long walk alone just to think. I'll not forget that walk since it was then I decided to take some evening classes to try to improve myself. I enjoyed writing and wanted to learn another language than English, don't ask me why. I was going to be nineteen years old shortly and had been after many jobs, but none of them seemed to hold much prospect of a future like the one I dreamed of. So I knew I'd better get with it and stop feeling sorry for myself if I wanted to move up. Most of the fellows I knew were in the same boat I was in, but they didn't seem concerned. They were mostly just interested in girls. And why not?

When 1939 came around, I turned twenty years of age (in January), and British law had it that every man of twenty had to enter the military for six months' service. Around April I got notification from the government telling me I had to go to the nearest Labor Exchange on June 30th and sign on.

By coincidence, the firm I worked for, Stanley Sports of Sydenham, decided to have a holiday on June 30th, the very day I was to sign in—boss's treat! We were all going to the coast at Margate in one large coach. Lots of girls, lots of fellows. And I was able to take my friend John (who had let me down the last year—you forget those things). I had my eye on one particular girl, so I was especially interested in going on the holiday even though it complicated my sign-up. I'd been told by the law I had to sign my induction papers on that Saturday morning, and I wasn't about to ignore that responsibility. That was the way it was.

Anyone who knows about England before the war knows that coach outings were glorious booze-ups, and any felicitations from the females were bonuses. And so about halfway to Margate, somewhere along the Kent coast, we pulled in to a pub and had a pint and bought another two or three cases for the road. Also during this stop we were able to move seats around and I could sit next to this girl I'd had my eye on. She had a friend, fortunately, and John was taken by her. So things looked good. The day was beginning to shine and we were all happy.

When we got to Margate, the driver pulled next to another pub—they want your business before, during, and after the day's outing. He pulled into a carpark next to the pub and we popped in and had another beer, and then we were taken by bus on in to the town center. I immediately started looking for a Labor Exchange office so I could sign up since I had to do it before noon. Luckily, I found one.

So I went in to find dozens of other men signing in. I didn't live in Margate, but I told the man in charge I'd been ordered to report. He said, "What do you want to be?" I said I wanted to sign up for the air crew, and he and some other men laughed and told me the air crew are full up.

"Well, then, I don't want to go in," I said. "I really wanted to join the air crew."

The man I was talking to looked like an ex-sergeant-major, and he didn't even smile. I thought I was being pretty funny, but he didn't seem to agree. He just said, "You don't have any choice. You're in. Sign here."

I was naive, and I said, "Okay, I'll take the other option. I'll go into the navy."

Another man said, "You're too big." (His idea of a joke.)

I said, "I'll go back to the air crew then."

He said, "No you don't. You won't get in. Besides, the navy's also full up."

I said, "Why are you asking me what I want to be?"

He said, "We have to."

I said, "Do you think I could get in the army or should I go home? I'd sooner go home."

He said, "Army? All right then. You're in. Congratulations." He'd known that all along.

I signed the piece of paper. Then I said, "Are you going to tell me which part of the army, which regiment, infantry?"

He said, "Whatever we can find you to do."

So that was it. I was going into the army. Before even going in the building, I was going in the army. I went outside and John was waiting for me, and we had a good laugh about it. Then we wandered off to where the sea was rolling in, and I forgot all about the army. We started talking about the day's future—never mind about the country's future. He just said, "Let's deal with today." That was all right with me.

We went along the waterfront searching for the two girls, and we came across them before long, and I knew we'd be all right. They'd had a few beers, and everything was okay. There was a fairground at Margate and we invited them to come along with us. It had carousels, swings, high sky dive, all those things, and we did the lot. They enjoyed it and we did, too.

We retired to the nearest pub. The girls had some wine and we had some beer. It was a good time. We had to be back at the appointed place to be taken to the coach, and we went to the back of the coach with the two girls, one whose name was Marjorie, and it was getting dark so we just snuggled a little bit in the back. It really was a good day without too much worrying about the future, just being tipsy.

We came home tired and said good night. It was really the end of my civilian life. I was in. No war was declared, but they would probably have called us up anyway for some kind of training or national service. According to the law, the calendar year you were twenty years of age was when you would be called. If you were junior to a man by a few months, he would go in first. That's the way it was done. I was one of the early ones having a birthday in January.

Off to War

The official letter from the government soon arrived, ordering me to Aldershot barracks for training on the 16th of September. England declared war on September 3rd. It wasn't easy saying cheerio to my mother and my brothers and sisters. They all made a joke of me asking for a measured uniform that would fit me as well as my suit. I promised to behave and told them I'd see them at Christmas time.

My mother didn't like it, of course. There were six of us children, and I was the eldest son. One of my sisters had just married. Three brothers—Albert, aged seventeen; Harry, aged thirteen; and Freddie, aged four—and one young sister, June, aged eight. They were at home. But I knew that, in a war, brothers may eventually go, too. That was a real worry.

There were already plans in Britain to have children evacuated from cities to small villages in the countryside so they could live with other children in other people's homes and be treated as family, could go to school, and hopefully could find life reasonably enjoyable and not too upsetting away from home. It was a good scheme and a much safer prospect than to leave the children in the cities, even though children were confused. Naturally, parents were upset and disturbed, but they mostly realized it was for the best.

The local authorities dealt with the planning and locations for the children to go to, an enormous project. My parents, remembering the first war, were terrifically upset, of course. Dad had been through that one and had been gassed. German gas canisters—hard to believe.

My sister June and my brother Harry were evacuated by train to a family down in a Sussex village where the man of the house was working on a farm. I didn't see them go as I was away in the army by then. Before I left for France I obtained some leave to go home and see my parents and family, and I went by train down there in the country to see Harry and June. They were delighted to see me and I spent a couple of hours with them, seeing the area and what they did for enjoyment. It looked good to me, and of course we spent some time with the "foster" parents and their children. They fed me, too, and I'll always remember the large plum pudding on the table. Harry and June must have told them it was my favorite dessert.

When I had to leave them, June hung onto my hand and cried. She wanted me to take her home, and I wanted to stay and help. Harry was good and took care of June, and the foster parents understood and eased it somewhat. I didn't tell Mum how hard it had been, but she and Dad used to go down to see them whenever they could, so I'm sure they knew.

My brother Freddie was born with a deformity in one leg, and it seemed he spent more time in hospital than at home. By the time he was fourteen, he'd had twenty-one operations on both legs. None of them worked. Because of the war, Freddie was sent away to the small county of Rutland, where children were sent who needed hospital care. The GI's from the U.S. who were stationed up there found out about the children and took on the care of them, with permission, of course. And every child ended up with a kind of godfather. (Our family has often thanked the man who looked out for Freddie.) I never saw Freddie until I returned home to England after nearly six years, and by then he'd become a young man, barely walking, the image of my mum, but with shoulders I wouldn't argue with.

Later in the war, Harry and Albert were indeed called up.

My dad was the most upset. He wasn't a man who showed a great deal of emotion. He was a good father, no two ways about that, but he didn't show emotion, neither great joy nor great sorrow. But he insisted on coming to see me off—I'd packed whatever was necessary for me to take, I was in civilian clothes and took a duffel bag and a heavy coat, and together we walked toward the buses about a quarter of a mile away. I didn't want him to come. I didn't want that parting. But he was determined to walk with me, and as we walked he started to say things like, "Why, why? We had the First World War to save our children, and look, now you have to go. Why?" and he swore. One of the few times I ever heard him swear.

We got to the bus stop. We stood there and I thought the bus would never come. Both Dad and I were looking all over the place for words, just to pass the time. The bus finally came along and I had to say, "I'll see you soon." I didn't know when. I just didn't know. War had been declared, so who could say what would happen. I just said, "I'll be okay, Dad," and he put his arms around me and I left.

1

LIFE AS A SOLDIER

I WENT TO ALDERSHOT—a military town, soldiers everywhere. I asked someone on the street how to get to the barracks. I found the head-quarters, went in and showed who I was, getting the usual routine that sergeant-majors do when you come in. They look at you as if you don't exist. They told me to report to the stores before I did anything else and get fitted out with uniforms and underwear. The sergeant-major—we came to call him Old Jonesy—looked at me with disgust as if I were a waste of his time.

So I went to the stores. Unfortunately, when I got there, they'd run out of uniforms and supplies. There was a war on, you know. All they had were heavy sticks that were supposed to represent a rifle. That's the truth. They had no uniforms, the new wartime battle dress, and they had no rifles. They probably didn't trust us with the rifles anyway; we were so green. So we were supplied with what I saw as a pick handle. It was that way at that time. I kept thinking: How can we win?

I hadn't the uniform, and neither had the other men who had regis-tered at the same time I had. We were all from different parts of the country, of course, with different backgrounds, and we had to report in to the barrackman, a Corporal Crockett, who told us, "That's your bed, and that's your bed," and so on. I think there were about twenty of us in the room. All of us confused and none of us used to sharing a room with strangers.

We were told to settle in, put our gear in the lockers, don't leave any money around—things like that. So we sat around, talked about what we were going to do, what we'd been doing, where we were from. We got to know each other a bit and any embarrassment was passed over pretty quickly. That's the way these things are. Everyone in the same boat. It was quite good, really. You hear all kinds of stories about lives, guys' adventures with the girls.

Corporal Crockett returned looking smart in a uniform made to measure. He told us to stand by our beds at attention. I don't think many of us even knew how to stand at attention except to pull our shoulders back. He told us we looked like a "shower of shit," and worse. He didn't spare any language, believe me.

Crockett told us the sergeant-major was coming and that we'd better look good; and of course Sergeant-Major Jones came in—*crash! crash!*—with his walking stick at his side, looking around the room with disgust—all an act—and he stomped around and stared at everybody. He couldn't talk about the state of our beds or the state of our clothes because they hadn't been assigned yet, but he'd walk around banging on things with his stick. He'd speak to each soldier with absolute disgust, speaking with disdain about everything: hair style, mustache—"little children's whiskers," he'd say, "trying to pretend he's grown up."

He came to me and I had longish hair because I always wanted to be fashionable, wanted to look like somebody that was a cut above normal. He stood in front of me—I'll always remember it—and looked at me as if I was taking up space. He looked me up and down. He'd already asked some of the fellows what they did for a living, and he came to me and he stood there—and I'm not very tall—and he looked at me for at least a minute. He was six feet tall. And he looked down at me. It appeared to take him a minute to determine what he thought I was. Eventually he poked me on the shoulder with his walking stick: "I know what you are," he said. And I thought to myself, I'm not going to say anything because whatever I say, I'll be wrong.

"I know what you are," he repeated. And I wasn't going to say, "What am I?" or "No you don't." So I just stood there and smiled, but that didn't work either.

"Shut your face," he said, and I hadn't said anything. "I know what you are. You're a film star. That's what you are."

I said, "Right. You tumbled me." That meant he worked it out. And that was insolence. I was taking the piss out of him.

"One more word—in the cellar," he said. So I shut up or I would have been in the brig until the old man came around the next morning. The company sergeant-major would have to let me out. I could be put on a charge, a 2-5-2. It means you're up before the old man, the commanding officer, or CO. "Dumb insolence" they call it. It means you're saying nothing, but your eyes give you away. I didn't know what he was talking about at the time, but I knew it wasn't good.

I managed to get by with that. He could have had me put in the clink for the night. He finally dismissed us, but we were told we were confined to barracks and were to be on parade tomorrow morning at six o'clock. A lance corporal stayed with us who would see that we didn't do anything that wasn't right. You could go to the toilet, but that was all. That lance corporal was an idiot. He had his stripe on his arm and he thought he was a general. He was a real dolt, but we had to do it the way he said: It was all about discipline.

So the next day we were on parade at six o'clock, and I remember it was cold, raining. The corporal told us to form three ranks. We didn't know what he was talking about. "Ranks?" What does that mean? A corporal had to show us a marching position. We just stood there. "Right dress!" We're all looking to see if we're level. "Front!"

Then Sergeant. Major Jones came out. He looked as if he'd been in a model's window. You couldn't fault him—his hair was exactly right, both sides, perfect; he's trim. It's six o'clock in the morning and he's magnificent. Had that stick under his arm. He always carried a stick. A classic sergeant-major.

He looked at us with the same manner as the night before and told us we were going to learn to march. It would last for two weeks. Parade duties every morning and barrack duties the rest of the day: how to walk, how to march, how to talk, how to behave. Within a week we were all the same. It was marvelous. It didn't matter how much money we had—we were all healthy, eating well, marching well, and living well.

We wore whatever we had: suede shoes or boots. Still no uniforms. They hadn't arrived. It was the same for everybody, so we didn't mind so much. Soon we started feeling the benefits of regular hours in bed, regular exercise, and regular solid meals. This went on for two weeks, and suddenly we had good muscles and we felt strong; we started to have pride in what we were doing. We wanted to be better than the other team. We wanted to be the best among the six or seven groups from different barracks. We wanted to be tops. Of course the NCOs— the non-commissioned officers like the corporals and sergeant-majors—were driving us, taunting us: "You've got to be better than those chaps," they'd say. It was like a race.

After two weeks we were reasonably healthy and were used to the discipline. You could start to which men would get further in the military. It was all in the character. Some of the fellows just stood up to the whole ordeal much better than others.

Special Training
Just before the last day of that part of our training, on a Friday, we were told that the following week we were going to go to another place not far away to get some "vehicle training." Vehicles? What vehicles? Tanks? Motor bikes? Trucks? Speed boats? We had no idea.

And we knew by then not to ask questions. We'd find out.

Our uniforms arrived later on that same day, and we were finally fitted out, although the uniforms were pretty far off from our actual sizes. I wasn't keen on being seen in such clothes, given my interest in looking good, but we all swapped around and ended up fairly well dressed.

They told us we could have the weekend off but we had to be back on parade at nine o'clock on Monday morning. So we all went to our various homes to do whatever, and of course my dad asked lots of questions. Mum asked if I was eating enough, the way mothers do. She said I looked smart but the collar seemed a bit large.

I wasn't sorry that I was in the service. The things I had been concerned about—money, job, status—were beginning to disappear as issues for me. I could see that my life wasn't going to be the same anymore and that being in the army was where I should be. Whether I was going to get killed didn't occur to me. I figured I was going to learn something about life that would benefit me after I got out, that I was going to experience something that might help me get a better living and a better look at life.

Dad asked lots of questions about what was going on, and he said it sounded no different than when he went in during WWI. He was in a cavalry unit, and he'd seen some action and had seen some fellows killed. He asked me what I thought about it all, and I said I was learning some discipline and that it wasn't hurting. It was making me more self-reliant and able to look at the future in a different light. I told him I was convinced that I could make something good of this. I knew we were in a war, and I knew it could be bad because of what happened in WWI, but I was certain that England—and myself—would come out of it better off. Of course I never truly saw it clearly.

I knew generally what had happened to my father but I hadn't been there. I'd only read about it; I couldn't experience it. It's impossible. Then suddenly our country changed. Overnight. Everyone was seeing war. It was really happening. And naturally everybody was concerned, especially the older people who knew about WWI. And my dad—he remembered. He said, "I only hope this mess will be over by Christmas. You don't want what I had." I agreed. "No, I don't," I said, but I didn't really know. Of course we know now that WWI was much worse, but neither was any picnic.

When I had my weekend off I was seeing fellows I knew who weren't in. My friends naturally wanted to know what it was like. We talked and talked about it. Everyone was intrigued: What do you do? How do they treat you? Where will you be stationed? It was all the buzz around London: The War. Most of the fellows I was speaking with knew they'd be going in soon themselves. If not, they'd be working on the war effort at home. But really, no one had any idea what it would become. Who could know?

When I got back to the base after the weekend, our platoon was late appearing for parade. Some of the fellows didn't make it back in time. They'd tried to stretch their weekend out just that much longer. That didn't go down well with sergeant-major Jones. He chewed us out every which way, but it seems he did it just enough to make his point. They were too anxious to train us to spend much time punishing us for such an infraction. He scared us, though. He was very clever. A good man.

Two transports came to the parade ground and we were allocated to one or the other of them. We piled in and off we went to our vehicle training. When we got to the training area, an officer came along and explained what we'd be doing: We were to learn to drive. He said anyone who already knows how to drive should step forward, and we had two men who stepped up. There weren't many cars around then, of course. Nobody had money for cars. So none of us but these two could drive. And they were made corporals, just like that. It ordinarily takes years to become a corporal in the army, but they made that rank in a day. It turned out that neither one was any good at driving. They either lied or they were the world's worst drivers. The corporal who'd been in charge was now below these two drivers. It was amazing. He'd probably served seven years to make corporal and now—it didn't make any sense. But war doesn't make sense.

We were there two or three days doing our vehicle training. It took a long time to get started because nobody listened. All any of us wanted to do was to get behind the wheel. Finally we were taken to all kinds of lorries. They'd apparently been commandeered by the army. They had just told people, "We want your vehicle," and that was that. Each vehicle had a qualified driver, an elderly civilian, who was supposed to teach us.

By the second day, we were driving these vehicles, civilian vehicles of all shapes and sizes but real vehicles. All trucks—some small, some big, some medium—all the vehicles we were going to be taught on. As I looked at all of them, suddenly I became nervous about what I was going to do. I thought, Am I going to be driving one of these? I haven't got a clue how to do it. You can usually pretend you know a little bit and get away with it, but I didn't know anything. If I'd known the consequences of volunteering, I'd have said, "Yes, I know how to drive," and I'd have been made a corporal. I think I knew about as much as the two who did volunteer. Anyway we learned all about manual engines, gears, brakes, wheels, size of the vehicle—all that sort of stuff. We sat behind desks and had a teacher.

The following day we saw the vehicles again and we were allocated to a certain non-commissioned officer (NCO) depending on which vehicle we were going to be taught on. I became petrified at the sight awaiting me. When the NCO asked for Mayhead, he was standing beside one of the biggest bloody lorries on parade that day, about five tons. The sort of vehicle you'd take for furniture moving or for a load of coal. Climbing up into it, I felt like I was going halfway to the moon. I thought the NCO was going to show me quite a bit. But when I got up there and looked, he spoke very gruffly, telling me how to do this and how to do that as though I was a bloody idiot. How I ever even got up into the driver's seat is beyond my comprehension. All I could see was this massive steering wheel and this huge seat and a long distance to the ground. And I was told to drive it as instructed.

I knew that I wasn't going to be very good. Of course I let the clutch out and the truck stopped immediately. And this NCO, he was fairly flashy, it got to him a little bit because he saw I was able to move it a few yards without stalling it. He said something like, "Well, at least you moved it. That's something." I finally got it into second gear and moved it slowly along, but all the time I worried about how I was going to stop it. I hoped he wouldn't tell me to stop right away since I didn't have a clue, and he didn't. We went along a road and took a right turn over to a small bridge. As I was turning I had to head over this narrow bridge keeping to the left without tipping off into the water, and I really just panicked, didn't know what to do, as soon as I realized where we were. The NCO quickly pulled up on the steering wheel or who knows where we'd have ended up. But somehow we got it 'round and straightened it up.

He told me to stop, but that wasn't easy either. And when I finally did he asked me to get down out of the driver's seat. We had two other fellows in the vehicle who were yet to get a turn behind the wheel, but I thought I'd done enough to stop my NCO from teaching anyone anymore for the rest of the day. At least he made it appear so by the way he spoke to me. I thought I'd better improve or I'd have to go somewhere else. To make a long story short, though, he stuck with me and, by the end of the week, I had learned to negotiate the truck well enough that I passed whatever test he gave me. The other two blokes were about as good as I was by then. None of us had ever even sat in a driver's seat, let alone driven anything.

Leaving Egypt

The day war was declared, everything changed. Men appeared from everywhere, seemingly overnight. We had troops from New Zealand and Canada and Australia. We knew the war was on and it was obvious that it would be big. Of course, there was rivalry among the nationals since some were getting better money than others, some had better uniforms, some were being treated better. I think the Canadians were probably the highest paid, and I think New Zealanders were probably close to them. We were the lowest paid, we British, I think.

They needed people urgently or I wouldn't have passed my vehicle test. After I passed, though, I didn't know what they had in mind for me. I thought I just needed to know how to drive, but I couldn't tell how that was supposed to help England win the war. At that time we were still green at the whole military system, still learning how to address people, how to follow military protocol. After a few more days, an officer and a sergeant came into the barracks and, after talking about what was happening in Europe, the officer tried to explain to us what we'd be doing. It was pandemonium on the front, he said. No one knew what was going to happen. Then he asked for volunteers to go to France. France? That sounded good to me. I stepped forward along with ten or twelve others. I wanted out of where we were, and this was the best offer I'd heard. I was surprised that the officer asked for volunteers, though, during a war. Why not just assign us?

We got set to leave in January, 1940. At that time, the Allies were in trouble. I volunteered to go because I just wanted to get on with it. We were sent home for a weekend, but we weren't to talk about where we'd be going. I went home and saw my parents and friends, had a nice break, and then went back to Aldershot. We were put on parade, addressed by an officer, and the ones of us who'd volunteered for France were called out. We were told we'd leave the following day, and we weren't to tell anyone. The regiment would tell our parents in good time. None of us understood the reason for the secrecy, but we naturally went along with it. Early the next morning, we were taken to the train station. As the train started moving, an officer came in and told us we'd be going to Cherbourg, in France. When we hit Southampton port, we met up with a long line of troops, all heading across the Channel. A military band was playing. There we were, among hundreds. We sailed late that night, in the dark, very slowly, and we got to Cherbourg in the early hours, and we were discharged to the town. We saw French and Belgian troops, but we didn't know the situation. We were put on parade early that morning, and none of us knew what we were supposed to do. We weren't allowed to talk about it to anyone, and really no one answered any of our questions.

Later, while we were still in Cherbourg, we managed to communicate somehow with the French and Belgian troops, and they talked about how hard they'd had it—no money, nothing. They were hurting. We bivouacked near Paris but we were told we wouldn't be staying there long, that we'd be going to Marseilles. What for? You don't ask what for, you just go. When we got to Marseilles, they said, we'd be told what to do. So that evening we were put on a train for southern France, about fifty of us. We were warned by the officers that Marseilles isn't a nice place. Thieves, skullduggers. We were warned to watch ourselves, to be careful, always to go out with a buddy, never alone. When we got there we were issued a tropical kit: sun elements, short summer wear. I never felt more ridiculous in my life.

They put us on a liner, the Duchess of Altholl, a Canadian-Pacific liner taken off its run, a luxury passenger liner. Ridiculous. I had a cabin with one other fellow. Here we were, about to sail across the Mediterranean in our own private cabin on a luxury liner. During wartime. The mind boggles at some of the things that occur. It was a strange war. Maybe they all are. We weren't told anything, only second-hand gossip. What were we doing in Marseilles? Who knew? We sat in the harbor until morning. I guessed we'd be going to Africa, since that's what made most sense; and that's what happened.

After a couple of days we sailed into Alexandria, Egypt. We came off the ship into a different world. The sun was burning on the city and the city was teeming with people we hadn't seen much of before. Funny little vehicles were everywhere. It really was a different world. We were taken to a camp in Alexandria, a peacetime barracks. We were fed and talked to by some officers who told us we were going to Palestine for basic training for possible warfare in Egypt and Libya. We departed from Alexandria by railway, and we crossed the Suez

Canal to Palestine for training to come back and fight whoever was in the desert—Italians, we figured. Of course we all felt that would be no problem. We knew we could handle the Italians. We figured we'd just go up there and take over.

2

THE MIDDLE EAST

AS WE ARRIVED IN HAIFA, none of us seemed sure about what was going on. We were transported to a training camp called Sarafan, about two hours outside of Haifa. It was a really peaceful camp. It had everything we could need. The British were serving the country and had taken charge, and we were taken to a barracks in battle dress that none of the peace-time regulars had ever seen. Of course all the old-timers laughed at us because of the clothes we were wearing and because of our ages. We were kids, hardly able to shave. The veterans made fun of us, had a real good time. They were okay, though, and we got over the jokes. They had mostly been trained to be Buckingham Palace spit-and-polish soldiers, but it didn't work that way now. In the Middle East we were drivers, armed soldiers. We drove armored vehicles, anything. We were sent to Haifa to pick up vehicles to be used in the training. So that was it for a while, until we started training for desert warfare.

They told us we'd eventually go to Egypt. The British knew the likelihood of a war in Egypt. We trained for the desert: digging in, disguising the land, hiding, creating phony camps, building phony petrol dumps, sniping, learning survival. Most of us regarded it as not too serious. It still seemed to us, ridiculous as this sounds, as though the desert war really wouldn't happen, as though we were simply preparing for someone's imagined fears.

But it did happen, of course. The senior service people knew what we were doing, though we didn't. The Italians finally declared war on England, apparently because England was losing and Germany was winning. The Italians wanted to go with the winners. So they sent us to Cairo where we prepared for desert warfare.

We stayed in Cairo for a few days then joined a huge convoy and went into the desert. There was only one road in, but we started to separate at a point called El-Dhaba. My company went into the desert in a unit of about 300 to 400 men. We were ready and loaded. The Italians came at us and attacked, but they weren't good enough. Poor machinery. They had some success, but not much. When Germany came into the Middle East, things changed. By the end of '41 and into early '42—by that point there'd been a great deal of fighting, very nasty—it seemed clear that there'd be a real battle in Africa. We were short of the materials we'd need, and we knew that. We chased the Germans back a bit, but when Rommel took over, they chased us back. This was real fighting, with tanks and mines everywhere. And the sand was merciless. The scenery changed constantly with all the sandstorms. Sandstorms were murder on your face and eyes, and on your weapons, so we were always bogging down. Because water was scarce, we used sea water to bathe and clean.

One morning there was lots of noise and hundreds of aircraft overhead, mostly German. The terrain was bleak with dirty sand everywhere, all of which was cut across with dry gullies the Arabs called "wadis" and populated with the occasional pieces of wild shrubbery. Scorpions scuttled around everywhere as we got ourselves ready to move farther up to the front. A few tanks were already moving, kicking up sand and dust and generally making our lives even more uncomfortable. We all cursed and spit out sand, not too happy about getting the grit in our corn beef and dried biscuits, and not at all pleased with the water in our dixies getting all curdled.

As we sat around waiting for the order to move out, a couple of old soldiers who had been in the desert a long time called some of us over to their area. We circled them as they dug around a bit and finally came up with a large scorpion, a mixture of green and pale yellow with those huge pincers and that quivering venomous tail. It looked more fearsome than a German with his horrible helmet on.

The two old campaigners then came across a long dark brown centipede with all its hundred legs moving around like mad leaving little pathways in the sand, and quite obviously the centipede was very excited and probably angry at what was going on. I felt it wanted to get underground or hide wherever it could, but I guess it didn't have much say in the matter once the men got hold of it.

One of the old fellows then drew off some petrol from a can and poured it gently into a circle on the warm sand about eighteen inches in diameter. Then, with a couple of sticks, they managed to pick these creatures up and put them in the circle. I certainly knew nothing of the habits of such beings, and God only knows what they lived on in this useless piece of territory, but then I was only a city man.

We wondered what the old-timers had in mind when one of them struck a match and set fire to the ring of petrol, and of course this sent those two predators into a huge panic or rage. They obviously wanted to get out and yet they couldn't, so for whatever reason they attacked each other. The two old soldiers started a betting game on who would win. I had to fancy those gruesome pincers on the scorpion and bet five lira on it. It was one hell of a fight. The scorpion had its stinging tail in the centipede more than once, but whatever the centipede had, he made it tell. The fight lasted a long time even though the fire went out. In the end, neither won. They both fought themselves to death. They were very tough and determined, and it's a pity they died. They should have been awarded the Desert Rat Medal. It was quite a sight to see and we talked about it for the rest of the day. Perhaps it inspired us in the rest of our slog up the desert. At least it made us think of how we all fight to survive, human or animal. What difference is there, really?

In the Desert

I was in the 8th Army—the Desert Rats. We got to the desert in September of '41 and I'd been there for six months before we hit trouble. There was a big push by the Germans and they completely took over the area. They'd come in with their Panzer Division tanks under Field Marshall Rommell, the so-called Desert Fox, to take over for the Italians. They moved so fast they cut us off. They surprised everybody. Officers and others were caught like little children. It was like these Rolls Royces shooting across the desert. It was bloody awful. I don't want this to sound too bad, of course, because I'm British and I don't like to point out that we were made to look bad, but the truth is Rommel was better equipped and better prepared than we were. It's as simple as that. We were really short of tanks and other materiel, particularly if we hoped to push the enemy back.

On one occasion, we were near Tobruk when we were told to try to get back to our unit as best we could. We got separated. We didn't fancy that much since it didn't look like it was possible to get back across German lines to our unit. An officer addressed us all and said it's every man for himself—that we were on our own. It did not make any sense to any of us. Must have been about 150 or so all in the same boat. No communication. I didn't like it. It was chaos. Enemy planes were flying over us and we knew the Germans were close. And we didn't really know where to go, how to get back to safety. It seemed rather hopeless.

I ended up with four other chaps. We had a vehicle, an armored truck, but we were cut off from the lines. We decided to go east and then south, hoping to avoid the enemy, the Germans. They weren't visible, but we knew they were near. We had to try to find our way out. This was the desert. There were no roads, and the weather could cause the scenery to change every morning. It really could. So there we were hoping we were going the way we wanted to go, but not really sure.

In the early evening hours, around eight or nine at night, I suppose, we saw a black mass heading our way, had to be one or more vehicles led by a staff car. A British officer got out and held a pistol at us and asked who we were. I was afraid he'd shoot first and ask questions later. He thought we were the enemy. It was a natural concern. The Germans had captured lots of our equipment and they were using it. The officer couldn't tell our nationality by looking at the vehicles. I told him we were on our way to back to our lines. "Don't move," he said. "This place is covered with land mines."

He introduced us to a major who was responsible for laying the mines. And he arranged it so this officer would see us through the field so we wouldn't get blown up. We were told to stick close to the staff car. This was rather dodgy, and we saw a few mines go up as we traveled. Eventually we stopped and the officer got out and said we'd passed the dangerous area and we were on our own. "Head in this direction," he said, and he pointed, and we took off, hoping to reach our company. We would need food and fuel soon, so we didn't have too much time. Fortunately, we found a deserted British lorry with lots of fuel in it, but nothing else, nothing to eat, so we took that and destroyed our truck.

Capture

And that's how we came to be driving slowly through that convoy of German tanks in the middle of the night, and how we were finally shot at and forced to scramble from our truck without knowing who was shooting at us. We did know, though, that our fellow British soldiers wouldn't be calling us Tommy. And of course we knew that other than the British, the main forces in the desert at that time were the Germans. So...

Finally somebody called out, still in English, "We are Germans and you are our prisoners. Come out with your arms in the air or you will be shot." Two or three blokes with helmets stood up with their machine guns. They said something like, "We respect you as British soldiers." Another man stood up and said, "You are our prisoners." One of our crew, a cockney named Andy, didn't want to give up. He was crouched next to me and he told me he'd be damned if he'd let them take him alive. I told him, "You suit yourself, but you can't win. You're going to get killed. If you want to do it that way, do it, but I'm going out." I'd never seen him before we'd got put together on the truck, except just around in passing. He finally, reluctantly, agreed to come out. It was a Hobson's choice, for sure.

So we surrendered. We came out of hiding with our hands in the air. It was the most helpless feeling I'd ever had. It's not a game like when you're a kid, but it's the real thing, a war, and these men are the enemy. You have to concede that they have beat you, that you are no longer a part of the battle, and you just hate to accept that bloody fact. We had learned to hate the Germans, to despise them, to want to kill them if we had the chance. And now we had to give up to them. It was horrible, and that moment would eat at my insides for the rest of my life.

It's hard to accept immediately that you no longer have any rights to dictate what you are going to do then or whenever. You have lost. It was particularly frustrating since we thought we had out-smarted them. It was hard to obey their order to put our hands in the air. We didn't, actually. We waved our hands to show that we had risen without rifles, but we wouldn't "reach for the sky." They seemed angry, but not perhaps as Hitler or Himmler might have been, stark raving mad. They were more like soldiers, maybe a bit tired—as we all were.

We asked the Germans where we were and they told us we were near El-Alamein. We had been off on our directions, but not too far off. We were a bit lost, but not bad. I think we'd have made it if not for this.

Very little was said. One German, seemingly to practice his English but probably to informally interrogate us, asked us questions like where we had come from and where we were heading, but of course we weren't about to give him any information. I told him with a straight face that we'd just left Camberwell Green, which is a place in London near where I grew up, but of course he didn't recognize that location out there. He didn't realize I was taking the mickey out of him. He spoke to his colleagues in German until an officer appeared. The officer ordered us to start marching, and after about an hour we were halted in a location with tents and vehicles and heavy armaments, and dugouts prepared for us. The troops seemed very interested in us and, like us, appeared dirty and unshaven. It began to sink in that we were really in the bag, that it was real. We'd been captured.

Soon a lorry came along with a German soldier driving and we were marched to this vehicle and told to climb in the open back. Before we left the area, though, a staff car showed up and I'll be damned if it wasn't Rommel himself sitting inside. I'd seen his picture, and there he was. He got out and started talking with the Germans in charge of the lorry. Then he came over to us and looked us over very slowly. He showed us no expression, no joy and no anger, nothing. He spoke to us in English, telling us that we were "the lucky ones" because it was all over for us. We wouldn't have to fight anymore, and we wouldn't die. I didn't feel lucky, and I'm sure none of my comrades did either. We were all too bitter and upset with ourselves to feel any sort of good fortune had occurred. Rommel wasn't as big as I had imagined, slight and fairly short. And he moved slowly, deliberately. But we were more interested in our survival than we were starstruck at seeing the famous Desert Fox.

We talked to one another about how to get out of this mess, about the possibility of escape. We were all shaken about the capture after our brief taste of victory through the mass of tanks the night before, but we decided to wait and find out where we were, how far we were from the coast, and how far we were from our lines before trying anything. We were angry at not having a compass which might have helped us know where we were, or more knowledge of what to do now that we were caught, and we blamed our misfortune on our own officers for failing to train us for such a situation. Of course we didn't blame ourselves.

I communicated to the German sergeant that we needed food and he waved his hands into the air as though to say, "You must be kidding." Some of the other Germans smiled when he did that and Andy felt that they were laughing at us, so he acted very polite and said, "Go f*** yourselves," with a big smile on his face. The Germans were apparently aware of this term and told him to shut up, but he had made his point. I still chuckle when I think of Andy's remark, and of his audaciousness.

Prison Camp

They took us to a place near Tobruk, and when we got near there, they put us into a makeshift camp. There must have been 10,000 prisoners of war there, Australians and Indians and New Zealanders and lots of others who'd been taken prisoner-of-war. This was a good place for a prison camp because it was surrounded by desert, essentially, and was cut off on one side by the sea. Barbed wire fences encircled the compound, and everywhere you looked you saw Italian guards with rifles.

I didn't recognize any of the Englishmen who were in the camp except for the group I got captured with. I don't know how they got there or where they came from. And I didn't know how many of our troops from my division got away. It seemed to me we were all pretty much doomed, but apparently some made it through. We heard rumours, of course. Montgomery wasn't the CO at the time. Things changed when Monty took over.

It's hell being a prisoner. I didn't agree with Rommel that I was one of the lucky ones, but I understood what he meant. I preferred the line of fire to the barbed wire cage. I found out later what happened to my unit. Most of them got back to El-Alamein and became fully mobilized. By then they could take on anyone. They were well trained and well equipped. When I was captured we really hadn't been looked after very well. There was too much going on in France for the British to equip the African troops properly. They needed it all there. So we didn't have what was necessary. We went without. That's why I was taken prisoner, in my opinion: No training for capture, escape, survival. None of that.

Montgomery came in at the right time. He developed a good name. He deserved it, but he was also lucky in his timing. He got terrific support: ships, American supplies, personnel, equipment, everything. By October, the British had over five hundred tanks in North Africa, and thousands of aircraft. They blew the hell out of the Germans. The Allies were scooting around the desert the same way Rommel had been chasing us down three or four months earlier. I was taken prisoner in June of 1942. Four months later Monty had taken over the 8th Army and they took the whole of Libya and Egypt in no time at all. It was good. I learned all this later, of course. None of us knew anything in the prison camp.

So my own unit survived and regrouped in El-Alamein, and they chased the Germans to the sea. In Algeria and Libya they gathered together and were in control. The 8th Army then joined the Allies in Italy and chased the Germans out of Italy, too. My unit was among them. I read all about it later. I could have been killed, of course, but at least I'd have been in on the action. My unit was artillery.

But I was a prisoner, and that's that, isn't it?

I was put in a big circular field with thousands of men—with men of all nationalities, all guarded by Italian troops. And we weren't getting food. We were hungry. Barbed wire fence surrounded the field, trigger-happy Italians guarding. We slept in the sand. We used to dig a hole in the sand to sleep in, to try to get some cover. We were cold at night, frozen. It gets very cold in Africa. No bathrooms, of course. We'd dig a hole in the ground for that, too. It was bad. Lots of men got very ill. Some starved to death.

Roughly ten thousand of us were held in this field. It's hard to know exactly how many. I was always hungry. Occasionally they'd throw some bread in among us and we'd try to get what we could. It was nasty. They wouldn't serve it to each person; they just expected us to pick up and scrounge for whatever was there. They fed us the way you might feed pigs, made us fight over a scrap of bread. Horrible. The men handled it well, for the most part, and didn't give the Italians the satisfaction of seeing any disorder in our ranks, but it wasn't good.

The Germans thought guarding prisoners was all right for the Italians but not for them. The Germans were fighters, not guards. We heard rumours, though, that they were having trouble getting the British out of Africa and into Italy, which was where they really wanted to keep us. They actually couldn't get us or themselves out. The Allies were bombing everything on the Mediterranean. I stayed at this camp for six months. New prisoners came in, but not many. I don't know if anyone tried to escape. I never saw it or heard of it. I don't know how anyone could have thought he'd accomplish it anyway with the barbed wire and all the guards. I also never saw any signs of panic from the enemy, either, as if they were chasing someone. The thing is, where would you go if you got out? You'd just be worse off. The desert was an unforgiving place. Go the wrong way and you'd die of thirst. They really didn't need guards to keep us in.

The four of us who'd been in the truck stayed together pretty much. Every few days we started noticing some guys being taken out and we'd never see them come back. We guessed they'd gone to a proper prison camp. Where we were wasn't really a proper prison camp. It was an unruly, stupid place. People just stood around with the guards surrounding them.

Blackness, that's what stands out about my time there. Black nights and days. Nearly all black. That I remember well. Africa was nasty. It was a black world there. The night was the worst because of the cold. No coats. No beds. Nothing. They gave us nothing. I was there from June to December with tropical gear. Nothing else. Same clothes every day. Never a chance to clean ourselves, let alone our clothes. We all had lice. I was lousy all the time. That led to madness. You'd see them under your skin, moving. Madness. Makes you do things you don't want to do. One morning I woke up and found the bloke next to me with a shoelace around his neck. He was trying to kill himself, for chrissakes. I shook him out of it and he seemed to get over that feeling. The place could drive you to that, though, no doubt. We'd all get short-tempered, but no one had the strength to back it up. Lots of arguments, but no fights, at least as far as I could see. We did get one issue of old uniforms one time, probably from dead foreign soldiers. Mostly more tropical gear, unfortunately. It seemed awful, but at least it was something. It was a change.

Jack-the-Lad

While I was at this desert camp I ran into a chap I'd known when I had been in Palestine. We were all just waiting for days to pass. We could hardly walk since everyone was so crowded in there, and we were too tired and hungry to do anything anyway. We just talked and got angry. So I saw this chap I knew. I remembered him because he was different. He had always dressed differently from the rest of us. And he got things. We didn't understand why, but he was better off than any of us. We didn't ask questions, just wondered. He seemed somehow privileged. He wore civilian clothes when I first met him. How? I didn't know. We were never allowed to put on civilian clothes, even when we went home on leave. That was the rule. We certainly couldn't do it in the barracks in the Middle East.

Even in Palestine, twenty miles from Tel Aviv, we had to wear our uniforms. And we didn't like to wear them because the natives didn't like us and we didn't want to stand out any more than we already did. It wasn't good. But this chap had been there for a while, and he knew the place and the people. He was what we called a "Jack-the-Lad," a person who just seemed to know his way around, especially with the women. I somehow didn't feel qualified to speak to him. He seemed senior to us, like he was an officer, even though he must have been about our age. We talked among ourselves, of course, asking about him. There were lots of rumours about him, but nothing was confirmed. He was seen as his own man—we didn't know how, but we all knew he was. As we got more involved in the army, we slowly felt more qualified to speak with him. He was taken ill while we were in Palestine, and he never returned. None of us saw him again while we were there.

Then one day I spotted him at the prison camp. I called my buddies. "You wouldn't believe who I'm looking at!" I had to keep staring at him. If I took my eyes away, I'd lose him. Too many people. I'm saying to my group, "Come over here." I pointed at him. "Who's that?"

They agreed.

I said to them. "I'm going over there." I thought maybe he'd remember us and perhaps he could help us. He knew his way around, remember, knew how to get the best of things. So I headed toward him, and my buddies watched which way I went so they could help me find my way back.

I got over to him, and he was sitting with two or three other blokes. I walked up to him, and he looked at me and says, "I know you. You were in Sarafan."

I said, "That's right." I said I hadn't seen him since he'd taken ill, and he said he'd been transferred. I said, "Everybody talks about you. How you been doing?"

"How does it look like I'm doing?" he said.

"How's your rations?"

"Like yours, nothing."

We talked a bit more about where he'd been and how he'd ended up in this hell-hole, and then I headed back. When I regrouped with my buddies I told them he was in trouble just like the rest of us. The next day I saw three or four Germans come into the compound, looking around. I'd seen them before, and they'd always just looked around and then left. But this time I watched them come in and they went straight to where our man was. I just watched. They bent over and talked to him. Other prisoners were around, of course, but they just talked to him. He went out with them. It was like he was under pressure. They held his arm and marched him out. I knew something was wrong. This guy wasn't the same as the rest of us. He'd once told us he had a Swiss mother. Maybe that was part of it. That's what we figured.

He went out and, after a few hours, he came back. Did it again on a couple other occasions. He always came back in as good shape as when he went out, so I figured he hadn't been mistreated. Once again I went over to him. "Are you all right?"

"Yes, why not?"

"Well, the Germans."

"Oh, that. I always get that because of my funny name. They think I'm a German. They can only take what you can give them. They're trying to use me. I always get a meal out of them." That was all he said, but we all knew something was wrong.

When I came home after the war, I looked him up and found he was caught and arrested the day after the war. Turns out he was a "Lord Haw-Haw." That's a name given to a traitor, a name based on a real man from England. Not his real name. Eventually the original Haw-Haw was arrested; the Allies found out he'd been a fascist. He escaped and became a broadcaster in Germany. He was a bastard. Everyone hated him. He was caught in the forest after the war. He was hated more than Hitler. Finally he was tried and hanged. It's what happened to this guy, too, our Jack-the-Lad. I learned years later that was caught after the war also, and he was hanged.

I never thought they'd hang him. I figured he'd found the good life and had sold his soul to get it. I've since read a book which refers to him. What he did was what I saw several times as a prisoner-of-war: These Fascists would come around the prison camps. They were usually former British soldiers wearing British uniforms with armbands, and they'd tell us how great it was to be with the Axis. They'd try to get us to join them. This chap was one of them. All those who got caught were hanged, I hear. We hated them. They had to stay outside the gates or the other prisoners would probably have torn them apart.

Life as a Prisoner

The main emotion you feel as a prisoner-of-war is that you're angry with yourself that you got caught. You just keep thinking, Why did I allow myself to get into this situation? You don't think clearly. You're on your own, no higher authority. In fact, if you're an NCO, which I was, you're responsible for others. You're constantly angry. You're treated like a sewer. You're nothing. And it hurts. You can't do anything about it except go along with it or commit suicide. People got shot because they'd lost concern about living, they'd just given up.

You can't keep clean. The movies about prison camps are mostly bullshit. I saw William Holden in "Stalag 17," and that was a great film. But everyone looked healthy. You really can't make a fit man look ill unless you starve the poor sod. This movie was entertainment. Some of the British war films regarding prisoners of war are downright ridiculous. You usually get well-educated men from Eton or Harrow, officers, all very healthy. "Look here old man, we can't have that." That sort of dialog. Stupid. Bloody lies. But you can't expect a film to show it as it really is because you can't make people look or be that way. We never had a haircut. We never had a bath. We were filthy. Our teeth were getting rotten. And the strange thing is that when you're in it and you see the men around you, you worry about them, not about yourself. You don't have a mirror, so you really don't realize just how bad you are. But you see the others deteriorating, and you worry.

As I said, the guards in North Africa were Italians. The Germans didn't like the Italians much. As far as the Germans were concerned, the Italians were only good for guarding and cooking. But at least the Italians seemed to recognize the Geneva Convention. The Germans didn't give a shit about it. That was a big difference.

The Germans usually laughed if you mentioned the Convention.

My limited experience in WWII was as a prisoner-of-war. I didn't know anything about the war except that we had to win it. I was interested, but mostly I just wanted peace for all. I didn't examine character. The Italians weren't well trained as soldiers. We also had prisoners of war among us who didn't know if they were coming or going. But in the war, if you were a prisoner-of-war, sometimes you hit a pitch, a particularly bad or particularly good time. My pitch, at least my bad pitch, was in Africa—Egypt and Libya. Without a doubt. For all of us, I'd say, it was terrible, just terrible. Anything after that was an improvement—that was, in a sense, a good thing. You had taken the shit life and you'd taken it because it was there and it was useless to try to fight it. You needed what strength you had for later. You always knew in your head that it couldn't go on this bad forever. Something had to happen. Something. You'd be moved, you'd get a new camp commander, new guards, anything. Of course, no matter how angry you became, you couldn't get into an argument with anyone. Why would you? The others were as bad off as you were. All we could do as prisoners of war was hold our heads up and march and take the mickey out of them as best we could. But it was still war.

We all had different habits. Cleanliness, especially. People have different standards, different ways of behaving, different ways of reacting to stress and pain and dirt. But you always knew the others didn't want to be there either, so that helped connect everyone. And one thing we had in common—especially the British: We never wanted to let the Germans see us quarreling. I can only say this about the Brits, of course, not about the other nationalities. As prisoners, we British were somewhat different to the Germans. We all felt this way, from what I could tell. I found it interesting that we were never allowed to mix with the other nationalities. They kept us apart, for some reason. Because of paper work? I don't think so.

So our attitude as Englishmen was never to let the enemy see that we were bothered. The Italians and Germans did their best to make us look disreputable, of course, to make us appear like tramps or beggars. "These are the scum of the earth": That's what they wanted to show.

But it didn't work from what I could see. I've seen the way French, Belgians, Czechs, others, were in Germany. The Nazis used anyone they could to do the labor so the Germans could go to the front. And we saw the way the prisoners were treated. They never succeeded in breaking the spirit of a single Englishmen, from what I saw. We were trained that way: Never ever let the Germans see you down. Basic rule of war for us. And each day when you had to go to work, like it or not, you always marched straight and wouldn't let them see you down. Pride. It's the way we are. No medals for that. I don't criticize others. They were our Allies, and how they handled the situation was their business. I only know how we behaved.

To be fair, we had to remember that the European countries were in the hands of the Germans; therefore the French, Belgians, Dutch, and others were handicapped. The Germans could harass the families of anyone who didn't cooperate. I didn't know how the Americans were, although I've heard lots of stories since then. The other Europeans never fought the situation, though, didn't even need a guard. But they were beaten, remember. Their families were at stake. The Germans occupied their land and had power over the prisoners' families. We were different. As far as I know the Germans always regarded us as the ones they wanted to get down. I understand a lot of it came from the First World War. So we had to keep this up. When we went to work we knew—it was unwritten—that we'd walk to work as though we were going on parade. Put on a show. Used to make the Germans mad. And we used to sing. That's the truth.

Leaving Camp

Every so often in the camp, a few guards would come in and call out some names. Those men would be taken away, and the rest of us didn't know where they'd go. But eventually the time came for us—that is the four chaps I knew and some others I didn't know. We were called to the middle of the camp and marched out. Some good distance, as I recall. We were glad to go. Anywhere was better than this. At least we might be able to get some food or to sleep in a bunk, something. Anything. That place was awful. I lost two stones—twenty-eight pounds—in the six months I was there.

We were ordered to climb in the backs of open lorries they had waiting. Probably about ten lorries in all. They beat at us while we were getting in, but that was all right because at least we knew we'd be getting out of that camp.

They drove us up along a coast road, through Libya. For whatever reasons, they'd stop along the way and we'd see German soldiers in their camps. The soldiers would stare at us as though they wanted to see what kinds of people they were trying to kill. They'd look us over with what seemed great interest. It was hot, and I was damned glad the trucks were open. We stayed in the trucks for four days or so, always driving by day and camping by night. We were going some-where, but we didn't really know where.

On the morning of the second day we climbed in after spending the night on the ground and we discovered that we had new guards. The Germans had put what were known as Sinusi in with us, which I understood to be a local tribe like Libyans, like Arabs. They wore Arab-type uniforms, and they were stone-raving mad. They were dan-gerous people to have on your lorry because you were liable to have your head blown off the way they played around with their rifles. Like they were toys. These were dangerous men. They couldn't handle the rifles. They were hopeless. They were the most dangerous people I've ever been around. And we had them with us for the best part of a week. It was a menace all the time. They never hit us, but they were crazy. Of course we had no chance of getting away from them. Lunatics.

I'll never know why the Germans agreed to this non-German type of procedure, allowing these men to guard us. The Germans are usu-ally so arrogant with their discipline. Perhaps they couldn't spare troops to go that far with us and get the trucks back. I really don't understand. I thought it might have been a job for the Italian troops to sort out, but maybe the Germans wanted to put us down somewhat. They didn't succeed, but I have to say those Sinusi guards kept us honest.

It was unusual to see people other than troops in this desert country. None of the camel and long-bagged tribesmen we might have expected. No doubt the war had them long gone. Our views were mostly of Italian forces, and not many at this stage. It seemed as if the locals were sent elsewhere.

The weather was hot and sultry with insects invading anything to be eaten or stung. The mosquitoes seemed a larger species than we knew back home, and of course many of us suffered with dysentery and other stomach ailments. We were in open trucks and could see what the terrain was like, where the enemy was hanging out, and what our chances might be for an escape. Not good. After a while we left the rough ground of the desert and got back onto the road not too far from the coast. This was the only time we saw buildings and life. The enemy were there and they must have known we'd be coming by and refueling. It seemed that many of them were fresh from Germany because they looked pale and young, and we became something of an attraction or them. We thought they might shout at us or make fun of us, insult us, but they just seemed bemused. Well, we probably didn't exactly look like the ferocious well-fed killers they perhaps expected.

We mentioned food once we stopped in the city, and the sergeant reported to someone senior and we were given bread and water, nothing else. But at least it was something. And of course to use a latrine you had to go in the company of guards who took us a few yards away behind a building. We had urinated in the back of the lorry during our trip.

This journey, as it turned out, was to Tripoli, and I estimated that we'd traveled about a thousand miles in the backs of those trucks. And when we got there, it was very quiet. We saw that part of the city was in good shape and was still quite attractive to people there who appeared to be tourists. Tourists? In the middle of a battlefield? The city was very clean and had its front line blue and sandy with old white-washed buildings. I had an odd sense of the irony of seeing normal people doing normal things, shopping and talking and drinking coffee. And here we were being held as prisoners with this horrible war raging all around the city.

On the Med

We were taken off the trucks and marched to the barracks where we were given food—bread and water. We stayed there overnight, and the following morning they took us down to the shore and herded us onto this boat, like a motor vessel with a top deck and cellars. A grain ship, actually, not made for carrying passengers. I suppose it was mainly a cargo boat. It was manned with an Italian crew which seemed to be shouting at one another—and at us—all the time. I guess they knew why they were there. It was a colorless piece of ocean transport. I seriously doubt that it was seaworthy.

We were hit with a pungent and horrid odor as we boarded, something like week—old dead fish—and the odor got worse when we were ordered down the rickety wooden step-ladder to the hold below. Just an ordinary hold for a grain ship. We couldn't sit down. We held each other up. It was the lot of us, a huge bunch, ten lorries full, all crammed into this tiny space. This ship had been worked on somewhat, but not much, in order to handle this human cargo.

There were two or three pieces of timber—two-by-fours, rough timber—joined to the side of the ship so they went out over the water. That was to be our toilet. A piece of wood joined the pieces to hold onto. You climbed out to use the toilet. If you wanted to jump from there and take your chances in the Mediterranean, I'm sure you'd have had no argument from the crew. They'd doubtless be glad to get rid of you. But nobody jumped.

The Italian crew and guards were very nervous on this ship. They couldn't calm down. It had the feel of a panicked ship. Once when I was down in the hold, suddenly the hatch was opened and all prisoners on deck were quickly thrown down. Then the hold was battened down—and that was it. Pretty soon we heard some airplanes overhead. The Italians had a machine gun mounted on the deck and we could hear it firing, but it didn't do them much good. The airplane—a British plane, I learned—was shooting at the ship. Thank goodness the Italians kept them at bay or we'd have all been drowned. Of course the pilot had no idea we were inside. We were lucky.

Once I needed to use the toilet, so I got up on deck and crawled out onto those rickety wooden bars just as two RAF fighter bombers came swooping right over me. There were two or three other prisoners out on the bars as well. The Italians started shouting and screaming, angry with us because we were out there. I'm sure they had their reasons for getting us in, but I don't know what they were. We managed to get back on deck and the Italians used rifles to push us down in the hold. We were happy to go. Then they shut down the hold and locked it. I heard later—another rumour?—that the POW ship which followed us was hit by the planes and over two hundred prisoners drowned.

3

ITALY

WE WERE ON THAT BLOODY SHIP FOR A WEEK. When we finally arrived in Italy, we were in rough shape. No food. Lucky to have water. We were put off the ship in Sicily. None of us really knew what Sicily looked like, but we realized it was an island. We were there for a day and a night after which time we were put back on the ship and taken into Naples. They marched us to a prison camp at Capua, near Vesuvius, the volcano. Of course we had no idea where that was.

This camp was a joy, relatively speaking. It was a well-run camp and obviously had been used a lot during the war. The camp had been a military training camp, and it had been converted to take care of prisoners of war. It was well organized, and we were treated surprisingly well. We were given a change of clothes, and that alone changed our attitudes. They had English supplies there from Switzerland. We were told to go into this barracks and sort ourselves out with army uniforms. We all wanted uniforms after the sticky dirty tropical gear we'd been wearing for so many months. So we just grabbed anything, whether it was our size or not. Just took it.

We actually received some recognition as human beings. We were allowed to take showers—albeit cold showers—with an actual piece of soap, and we saw our brown, bearded faces in a mirror for the first time. We even got shaves and haircuts by one of our men who had been a barber before the war. The Italians actually trusted him with razor blades. We didn't look great, of course, but it didn't matter much. We were clean and we started to smile at each other again. We shook hands and even laughed a bit.

It was on that very day, having come through so much together, that a bond began among us which lasted throughout the rest of the war. We hoped we could share more time together until we were parted, and we often laughed about meeting in London after the war ended and how we'd get drunk together in a classy hotel with girls sharing our repatriation.

We enjoyed the spaghetti we were given and the heavy coffee, and we all fell asleep on small bunks provided for us. It was heaven that day and night. The next day some Italian doctors checked us all over and they gave out some medication for those who needed it. And most of us needed it, to one extent or another. It was fair treatment, especially considering how bad life was in Italy for the Italians themselves.

The Swiss were appointed by all countries to be the visual attendees of prison camps. Swiss officials were like customs men, and they came to the camps and notified the commanders of their appraisals. I know the Italians and Germans were afraid of these people. They really were. Whenever they came to a prison camp, you knew about it a week before because the Italians had you make the place look all spruced up. They wanted to appear tolerant and fair. I'm certain that the Swiss representatives knew exactly what was going on.

You seldom heard the Swiss observers speak when they were there, and they were always accompanied by German officers. Prisoners weren't allowed to speak to them, of course. They were the people who supposedly organized the Red Cross food parcels. I just remember them driving around in big cars with Red Cross insignias on them, but I don't remember them ever doing us any good.

There were lots of prisoners already at the camp in Capua when we got there, and they were all better dressed than we were. Better fed, too. The Italians seemed to care more about the humanity of a prisoner. Of course you have to understand that the Germans were always in charge, no matter who was supposed to be handling us. The Germans were always outside the gates. But we officially became Italian prisoners of war. In my experience—and I was in four different camps—I concluded that the Italians, as a rule, treated others—especially prisoners—far better than the Germans did. They paid attention to the Geneva Convention. They took care of the sick.

If you were in a country with soldiers getting hurt, you'd have to expect that the country would take care of their own first. But if you got sick, you should expect decent treatment. The Italians were reasonable. I wouldn't knock them as commanders or guards. You always get some idiots, of course. In England, too, we have our idiots. But generally speaking, the Italians were honorable and humane. No question about that.

I had at this time what one could call a "good" period. Compared to the early months in North Africa, this was relatively comfortable in as much as we could keep clean. That was a major treat. We had water. It was cold, but we could still have a shower. There was a long pipe going along the room and it had holes in it. So when the water came on, a half dozen fellows could stand under it at the same time. It was about five feet up. Cold, but you felt better for it. So that was that. It was a shower of sorts. Being clean ranks high when you're in a prison camp.

We slept in bunks inside. That was also a treat. It appeared to me that this was a good camp because it was a transit camp, one to welcome prisoners into the country and then sort them out to send them to other camps. It had trained staff who knew what they were doing. They gave us blankets. We slept on a *palliase*—a long blanket with straw. That was the mattress. That was on pieces of wood. Much better than digging a hole in the desert sand.

In camp during the day we just walked around. Everybody in prison camp life just walked. The walking provided exercise and diversion. When you first go to a camp, you have nothing except what's in your pocket. Nothing else. A pen, maybe, or some money. A handkerchief. You aren't entitled to keep anything. The guards would just take it. As a prisoner, then, you become like a magpie. You steal anything. Anything. If you have a watch, you hide it. The guards would take it away. A ring? Hide it. You had nothing. You might want a piece of string for a boot lace. You keep looking. You always look. You become a full-time thief, of sorts. But you never steal from another prisoner. You have to live with yourself. I never experienced it or even heard of it happening. But you'd always look for something.

In Transit

We didn't stay there long, unfortunately. We were in transit. As I recall there were nothing but British at this camp. Some were in full uniform. Officers were never with us. I can't recall seeing officers in any camps or boats or anywhere. Sometimes it was policy to get rid of insignia because the officers were treated differently and didn't want to let on their rank. But I never was aware of any officers among us. The officers had their own camps, separate from us (except in Africa where they threw us all in together). We were only at Capua for three or four weeks. That experience made us think prison camp life wasn't so bad. We were always hungry, but we were clean.

Then some of us were told we'd be going to another camp called #53. We were shipped out on lorries and taken to Camp #53. It was a big place with lots of Italians as guards. Some even spoke English. It was too full, though, that was obvious. Overloaded. I was there for a couple months. I occasionally saw others—one was an NCO, I recall—getting called out and given instructions, and then they were sent away. We didn't know where they were going. There was always talk that they were taken out and shot just to cut down on the numbers. No one knew. Rumours flew everywhere. I later learned that they were sent elsewhere to work camps.

Then of course it happened to us. My name was called out and about twenty other names. We were told to go outside and wait, just stand there. The guards gave us a package of food in paper, like you'd get in a shop, and told us we'd be going to another camp, but they didn't tell us why or where. There was a definite change in attitude, though. They were much firmer, less congenial than we'd come to recognize. We were checked out to see that we had sufficient clothes, and then we were marched to a railway crossing. Not a station, just a crossing.

The train arrived, not a very big train, probably only half a dozen cars or so. We couldn't speak Italian but we knew to get on the train. We'd always been crammed into spaces like cattle before, but this time we were taken to compartments, like civilians. I was told I'd be in charge since I was the NCO, and I told the men it looked to me as though they were making up to us a bit. They were certainly treating us a lot better than they had. Naturally we wondered why they wanted us, what they expected us to do. We didn't know where we were going, not even which direction. We worked out that we were heading north, but of course we didn't know how far north we'd be traveling. We passed through Rome, where we stopped for a short time before departing that station without getting off. Where were we going? Perhaps the Italians with us didn't know either. After Rome, we traveled for hours and didn't pass any towns, only fields and forests, more fields and more forests. So we knew we were heading for the country.

We all agreed we were probably heading for a work camp. There were twenty of us, including myself, on this clean and tidy train; we were actually comfortable for the first time in months. At about five in the evening, the train made a stop by at a small crossing and the guards ordered us to get off. We still didn't know where we were, of course, but the guards started us out on foot up a dirt road into the hills. The area was quite beautiful, filled with lush green growth of various vegetation. And the smells practically made my head swim. I couldn't believe that we'd be so fortunate as to be able to work in such a wonderful locale.

A Different Kind of Camp

Then, for the first time in my life, I saw rice growing. We looked off the pathway into a field and saw this strange crop. The truth is, none of us recognized it; we'd never seen rice fields in England. Naturally we were curious about it, wondering mainly what it was, but we were more concerned with our futures at the time: Where were we heading?

The guards from the train weren't helpful, of course, but they didn't do anything really unkind or out of line. They merely marched us for a few miles at a steady pace, and soon we were marching past one rice field after another. It was quite exciting for us, actually. The situation didn't look menacing. It didn't look like anything we needed to be afraid of. Walking along this pathway in open country as we were, I could not help but think how good it was to be there after all the time in those camps. No barbed wire, no sand, no lice, no digging holes in the ground to defecate, or to sleep. Here we were surrounded by green: All around were fields. Fields, fields, fields.

As we came around a long bend in the road, we heard women's voices. Naturally we looked out across the fields, and there we could see female figures with big straw hats on. About all we could see were their heads going down and coming up. Down and up, down and up. Turns out they were planting rice, but at the time we didn't know what they were doing. We'd never seen it before. We could barely hear their voices as they sang together, not knowing we were there. As we approached, we could tell that they were actually singing in harmony. When they finally became aware of us, though, they stopped their singing right away and we could tell they were frightened. They'd undoubtedly heard stories about us English being a bunch of gangsters and hooligans. Basically the same things we'd been told of the Germans, they'd been told about us.

The guards worked out where we should walk without destroying the fields or getting too close to the women. We crossed the rice paddies, but we could hardly stay on the path since we were so focused on the women working. We made a few remarks, of course, that the women could hear but didn't understand, the usual flirtatious comments. The guards marched us right on by them to the edge of a field and through a gate into a small country lane. In the distance we could see one or two buildings and a church. This was actually a very small village named Monticello.

The guards would occasionally speak to us, but we seldom understood them. We gathered from their gestures that we were to walk through the village and that we were to keep silent. They took us right into the village square and it was very dull, not really inviting, quite gray. The square was surrounded by some shops and a church. All the people had gone into their homes when they found out we were coming, and they had closed the windows. They'd heard stories about us.

The square was the focal point of the village. It branched off into five lanes, each a pathway of its own and each leading to a different farm. There were five farmers. Everything of significance that happened in the village occurred in the square: weddings, funerals, celebrations. People met there every day and talked. We didn't understand at the time what our jobs would be. It was all new and different for us. But at least it wasn't the desert.

Duties

A uniformed man arrived as we were congregated in the square, and he looked like an officer but he was really a senior NCO, a sergeant-major. He approached me and told me as clearly as he could, without speaking English, to introduce him to the men. Right away I felt he was a fair bloke. He then told the guards to take us to our quarters, and he told me to assign beds, assign work teams of four men each, and assign a cook. I was then to report to his quarters, located right next to the house we'd be staying in.

So I spoke to our fellows and told them to make up into gangs of four. I wanted them to make up their own teams. I told them I'm going to have to tell the Sergeant-Major which four would be where. Everyone cooperated. The Sergeant-Major had told me that we'd start working the next week. This was a Saturday, and we had to be at the square on Monday. We were then marched to what we thought would be a prison camp, but it wasn't. It was really just a house, an old house which had been refurbished to accept prisoners.

The house had outside steps. We were taken to what they called the courtyard, actually just a garden area, covered with dirt, though, not grass. A wall with barbed wire surrounded the entire house, including this courtyard. This was where we'd live. Naturally we immediately started talking about escaping. It certainly looked possible.

I had to explain to our guys what I thought the Sergeant-Major tried to tell me: Work on Monday morning. Meet with the farmers. Agricultural work—which was within the Geneva Convention since it wasn't work toward the war effort such as manufacturing bullets, making shells, things like that. I had tried to ask what kind of agricultural work, and the Sergeant-Major just said, "Rice." None of us knew what that would be, exactly, since we'd never worked in a rice field.

Of course there was some bickering about who would sleep where. On which floor. First floor or second? We were all in the same house and each floor was made ready for people. With bunk beds, new straw mattresses. We had four guards and bars on all the windows and the door. The house was surrounded by a small moat, more like an irrigation ditch. We finally agreed as to who would sleep upstairs and who'd sleep down. Of course, some blokes didn't like being told what to do by me, and I avoided that whenever possible, but I was the NCO, so sometimes I had to do it. We were all prisoners of war, though, and therefore all equal. What could I do if they didn't like something I said? I didn't know. We were told where to live and I was to sort out the assignments. Simple as that. I tried to be easy about it, though, and the others went along.

The main problem I faced, actually, was that I had to find a cook. Who wanted to be a cook? Well, everyone wanted that job. The thought of being in charge of the food after being hungry for so long was really appealing. Why not? The guy I finally assigned was a young bloke who'd said he'd been a cook before. I said, "You want the job?" He said, "Yeah." So I said, "You got it." He was happy as could be, just what he'd wanted. A couple others also had asked for the assignment, but this fellow had told me he'd had some experience, so I went with him.

Sometime later the Sergeant-Major arrived to check up on us and I told him what we'd done. I said we had a cook but that we needed some food. He got bread for us right away, along with some cheese and fruit. So we all had food to eat. He told me to come to his office and we could do our best to talk about things. Some of the blokes didn't like my going in there, of course, but I didn't see any harm in it. Since it had to do with our future plans, I felt I had to find out. Don't know how I could have said no, anyway, frankly.

I'll never forget my first visit to the Sergeant-Major's office. He closed the door and offered me a glass of wine. Wine! Then he looked at me, shrugged his shoulders, and said, in Italian, of course, some-thing to the effect of, "This is war. We may not like it, but this is how it is." He asked me my name, and I said, "Charles Mayhead."

"Charles?" he said. "Charles?" Then he smiled. "Oh, Carlos!" And he shook my hand. "Gino," he said, and I realized he was telling me his first name. Yes, I thought, this is a good bloke.

He went on to explain that he didn't want to be there any more than I did, and that if we helped him he'd help all of us. If we made it tough on him, though, he'd get tough with us. He made that clear. I said I'd tell the others. I figured that was a good way to go.

Starting the Routine

This was in the early spring of 1943. I'd been a prisoner about a year by the time I got there. By this time the Americans were in the war, of course, and it looked like the Italians would lose, although we knew nothing about all this except the few rumours we'd heard. Nothing had been substantiated. We could see, though, that the Germans were animals toward the Italians. They regarded the Italians as nothing. The

Italians weren't having a good time in this war, and they clearly wanted out. The Sergeant-Major didn't say all this, of course, but we prisoners all talked about it, and I learned about it later.

We had the rest of Saturday night and all day Sunday, and we'd all had something to eat and had decided where to sleep. This seemed like a good start. Sunday arrived—a nice day, I remember it well—and we had very little to do. We weren't asked to go to church, of course. They didn't want us in their church. We all got together, though, and talked about our situation. I said, "You guys can escape if you want. I realize it's our duty." But I suggested that we shouldn't do it until we knew just where we were. None of us really knew where we were. It turned out we were fairly close to Milan, but we didn't know that then. Besides, we would have to get fit if we ever wanted to succeed at such a plan since we were all pretty weak. Plus we knew there were dangerous Italians all around. Fascists. At least that was the word we'd heard. Rumours.

We were given some more food. Our cook, this young bloke from the north of England, put together a soup for us out of rice and tomatoes which, along with fresh water and bread from the village, made a great feast. That was his first meal, and we were all impressed. We felt nearly human again, sitting around with an actual meal, talking and laughing. This was such a far cry from the earlier prisoner-of-war experiences that it seemed to be another world entirely. War? What war? We could as well have been farm laborers in southern England.

On that Sunday afternoon, what happened in that village must have happened throughout Italy. Young women were able to register with the regional farm association and go pick rice to take home to their families. It was similar to what we called a "poor man's holiday" back home, although in England we picked hops for beer rather than rice for food. So these women were in the village to gather rice. They'd been in church in the morning, but they were free in the afternoon.

We heard noises outside and climbed on the beds and looked out the windows through the bars. The women were gathered across the ditch just sitting there talking, giggling, obviously wondering about us. They must have thought we were wicked. We were all a bit randy, of course, and hollered out at the women, whistling and making gestures. Each of us got right to it and picked the ones we liked.

There was one woman who was quieter than the rest, and to me she was very attractive. All our guys were yelling, "Hello Senorita! I love you!" and "Cigarette?" and "Wanna get married?" The usual stuff. Of course the women didn't understand the language, but they certainly had to understand the sentiment. I was the quiet one among us, as this girl was among the women. I looked at her and waved, and she smiled.

We moved to the back yard, and we spoke to them through the fence. The women were just across the ditch on the other side of the road, only about twenty or thirty feet away from us. It was a real experience. These girls were from the towns, not from this small village, and they'd seen a bit of life. They knew how to flirt with a man. And, being a Sunday, the village was dead, nothing else going on. So there was a bit of laughter from both sides.

After that, of course, we couldn't wait for Monday. We knew these girls would be working on the land and we thought there might be chances that we would see them. We'd already decided who would work which fields on that Monday, and there was no changing that. In the morning on Monday, one of the guards let me know that I was to go outside the gate to meet with the Sergeant-Major. None of us knew what was going on. The Sergeant-Major informed me, as best as he could, not to let the guys touch the girls. If so, we'd all be in trouble. He wouldn't put up with it. We had a good talk. He said we were to do our best and have as good a time as possible, but not to try anything funny. What could I say? I told the guys, and they weren't pleased, but they seemed resigned to the situation.

He'd assigned two guards for each group of four prisoners, and each crew went out onto a farm with the farmer who owned that place. Sixteen of our colleagues were out of sight, and I was with three chaps I didn't really know. We wouldn't find out what the others did until we got back to the barracks that night.

The guards marched us along the path and then, suddenly, into deep muck. Wet, muddy, it sucked us in. The women were there in the field we were assigned to, about thirty of them, working the rice paddies. We thought we were in heaven. The farmer tried to explain what to do, but we didn't understand what he was talking about. He tried his best to show us while all we wanted was to work near the women. Clearly, though, we were to have nothing to do with the women, and the guards were sitting with their rifles on their knees to remind us. Pretty frustrating.

This shy girl at that field caught my eye. I spotted her right away. I asked her name. I told her my name was Carlo, in Italian, and she seemed to get a real kick out of that. She was Christina. In the next few weeks, we all managed to find ways and means to communicate to the ones we'd had our eyes on. I made all sorts of promises to Christina across the field whenever I got the chance. "When the war's over we'll get married," I'd say, and we'd laugh. I spoke to her every time the opportunity arose. She was very reserved, though. I could hardly see her face. I tried to explain to her that I hope she understood we hadn't spoken to a woman for a year or more.

Problems with the Cook

Working around the women helped us feel like we were human beings again. Just being there, making comments, having eye contact, just hearing their voices when they sang. It gave us something to get up for. The cook, of course, got to hear about this, about what went on in the fields. It wasn't easy work out there, but at least we got to visit with women once in a while and got out in the fresh air. We weren't looked on so much like the scum of the earth, the way we'd been in other camps. We also felt that we were teaching the Italians that the British weren't monsters as we'd been depicted. That was a good principle. Of course the cook was eating well, but he was alone all day with nothing to do but prepare the next meal and clean up from the last one. The rest of us were together and going out and having adventures. This started getting to him, even though most of us were breaking our backs in mud fields.

It wasn't long before he wanted a change. But I wasn't responsible for making changes. That was for the Sergeant-Major to do. The cook, frankly, became fed up with what he was doing. It was all right for a while, but he soon tired of it. It was a one-hour job every day, and then nothing. He just looked at himself for the rest of the day. So he came to me about the change. All I wanted, of course, was the best deal we could get. We should work and get fed. That was primary. If he got his change or not, I wanted to be sure we all continued with our work and meals.

When I got back from work each day, I was to report to the Sergeant-Major's office to tell him of the day's activities: what we'd been doing, what complaints there were, what we needed, all that. Sometimes he'd give me a cigarette or a cup of coffee and we'd talk, as I was learning Italian. I always looked for something that might help the men. The whole meeting would take ten minutes or a quarter of an hour. Then he'd get the guard to take me back to my quarters.

As a result, I would arrive at our quarters later than the rest of the fellows, and everyone else would have already eaten. And I became aware fairly quickly that the cook didn't like what was going on, didn't like my coming in late for the meal. I didn't know why he was so upset, but I knew he wasn't happy. He thought I was getting something I shouldn't have been getting, I suppose, and he had one or two moans about what was happening, muttering something about privileges. So I came in one evening and just as I came in through the gate he started yelling at me. Something like, "You're late again, Mayhead, and if you come in late you'll get no food." It was ludicrous.

When you become a prisoner-of-war, it's very difficult to use rank, because you are no better than anyone else. You're all prisoners. I'm sure it's the same in all nations' services. You could be a corporal and who would care? Who would enforce any military discipline? But the way I saw it, if you were in charge of a group, regardless of rank, you were in charge. That's the same everywhere. If one of the men does something wrong, the NCO is supposed to rebuke him. You never put the man on a charge, but you try to end it by saying, "Cut it out, you're being silly. If you don't, I'll put you up in front of the old man when we get out of this." Which you can do if you have the guts.

And if you have the authority and know the book of rules, you can say to that fellow, "I'm ordering you to...," and the guy might say, "You can go screw yourself," or whatever. You can then say, "That's it. You're on a charge," and he might laugh at you and ask you how you're going to carry it out. If you know the book of rules, though, you just point and say, "You're there. You're under open arrest. After the war, you'll go in front of a court and you'll have to answer." That's just strict rules.

In this case, I immediately felt myself get angry at the cook's comments, but I decided I'd try to ignore him. He wanted to do away with my rank so I couldn't do anything about it. I was a bit hot under the collar, but I kept quiet and started to walk upstairs. And he didn't seem to get it. So he repeated what he said about my getting no food if I came in late. I just stopped, turned, and looked him in the eye, and I said, "Oh yes I will." That's all. And I walked upstairs. He didn't like it. I think I didn't say enough to antagonize the situation the way he wanted it. I was halfway up the stairs when he shouted out something to the effect of "You and your rank—piss off."

As an NCO, I have no right to touch him at all, any more than he has me. But I would be worthless if I let it go. I couldn't take this because he'd said it in front of about six chaps sitting there eating their food. I could ignore what he said and carry on or I could react and show him who I was. And that's what I did. I had an advantage over him because I was on the stairs, higher than he was. So I asked him to repeat what he said. He shouted out that I should come down the stairs and he'd knock six kinds of shit out of me. He made a mistake, though, because I was angry. I started down and he attacked me coming up the stairs, so I had the momentum. I leaped onto him and immediately knocked him down. Then I hit him and hit him again. We tumbled down the stairs onto the ground floor. He had no chance, considering the situation, but I'm not proud of what I did.

I was stupid to allow myself to get involved. But I know that I was getting out a lot of my feelings about the war. I was mad at life, and he was the person who got what I was feeling. I don't regret that I hit him. But it was silly hitting one of your own in a prison camp when you really wanted to be fighting the enemy. I knew I had to act, though, under those circumstances.

Fortunately another bloke jumped over the railing and grabbed me. He stopped me, pinned my arms back. I was angry, don't know when I'd have stopped. I was a five-minute hero to some of the fellows, but I didn't need it. I didn't need any of it. I hated it. What I felt was I hope this doesn't last. He could have had me court-martialled. He finally had enough sense to stand back and say to me that he wanted to get off cooking. I said I couldn't do anything about that, but I'd tell the Sergeant-Major.

The Sergeant-Major found out about the fight and he called me in to ask me about it. One of the guards was just outside the gate and watched the whole thing. The guard had shouted, but he hadn't approached us. It was over pretty fast. I'd have probably attacked him too. I was blind with anger.

I didn't want to get involved like that, but I had nowhere to go. I had to deal with it myself, and I dealt with it wrongly. But I got rid of a lot of anger that I was feeling. I didn't want to be a soldier in a prison camp. I was just angry. I don't like this episode. It's just anger. I let life get the better of me.

I had been going upstairs to clean up and had planned to return to get my food. The cook had a fire outside where he was cooking. Most of the time our meals consisted of local bread with soup. What was in the soup, you could only guess—mainly rice or pasta and polenta, I suppose. The cook really knew no more about cooking than I did. I thought at the time he was good enough, though, for what he had to work with.

Having said all this, I must point out that we were all good soldiers, and we'd seen our share of action in the Western Desert. We were keen to get back to the lines and carry on helping to finish this war. But to be honest, we were feeling that someone was looking down on us and giving us a little break by assigning us to this camp. We didn't want to stay in the camp but only to use it until we were in fair shape and found a way to escape in the right direction in fair shape. We learned that Milan was fairly close and we also knew that Milan was not too far away from the Alps, and that just beyond that was, eventually, Switzerland. If we could get to Switzerland, although it might mean internment, we would have a chance of escaping.

We had to get up fairly early. Up by seven and out by half past to get to work by eight. It was quite a walk to the fields, which weren't next to the village. We had usually had some coffee and bread by the time we got to the fields. We'd work until one or so then get a half-hour break. If we were lucky we'd get a bowl of rice from the farmer during the break, maybe even some cheap wine. In the evening we'd have a meal, loosely speaking. Whatever was given to the cook. All the European countries were in trouble with food, even for their own people, so we prisoners were the last to be considered, but you'd expect that.

Italy was in serious trouble in terms of subsistence. So much of the country's energy and money went into the war effort that the people ended up having to fend for themselves. In the villages, people naturally looked after their own. We were fortunate. For the first time since we'd been prisoners, we were having food each day. We were outdoors and exercising and breathing fresh air. And we could always find something to eat. In the previous camps, there hadn't been anything so we considered ourselves lucky. We were almost like civilians. We had guards, of course, but we were lucky. I don't think the Germans would have treated us this way.

Sandro

One time I even had the opportunity to work with a horse in the field.

The horses were mainly used to pull the loads of rice from the fields. Remember that when you are in a rice field you are in deep oozing mud, and it seems to get worse each day. Sometimes you lose your footwear because it gets stuck deep in that muck. It's that bad. Anyway, I felt one of the horses was overworked. I'm sure it had kind of arthritis because walking seemed hard on the old nag. He was a huge animal, seemed to a city boy like me to be the size of an elephant. His legs were like oak trees and were all gnarled, and he never seemed tidy at all. His name was Sandro. I used to look at him and want to go over to him and say something to him, perhaps give him something to munch on. He seemed so lonely, with his head always low as if he wanted to spread out on the bank side and just snore away. The horse gave me something to think of other than camp life.

The man who was in charge of this horse was one of the farm hands named Renato. I always remember him as the man who talked to me whenever he could, and he once told me that he only had one testicle. I said I was sorry about that, and I tried to extract some humor from him by adding that he should pay more attention to his horse because I felt that poor old sod hadn't got any left, the way they worked him. He laughed and said, "No, no, Carlo. Sandro *forte* (strong)!"

I replied in my rough Italian, "Bullshit." He understood, I'm sure.

One day Renato came over to me as we sat with our two guards for vino and bread, and he asked me if I wanted to see where Sandro spent his evenings and nights, and of course that would be welcome to me, anything for a change. So there was much chat between the guards and the farm foreman and, at the end of the day, we were all marched back to the camp, as usual. I had to talk to our fellows to find out if anybody was sick or suffering, how the food was, that sort of thing. Then, as was the routine, I reported to the Sergeant-Major.

To my surprise, the Sergeant-Major said that he understood that I was interested in Sandro, the horse, and that I thought it wasn't being looked after properly. I didn't know how to respond except that I thought the horse was tired out there in the field and his legs didn't look good. The Sergeant-Major looked at me with a little smile and said, "So you think we are brutal?"

I hedged it a bit, but said I only thought Sandro needed a trim up and a hot bath. He opened the door, and there was Renato. They talked a bit, and finally, with a guard, Renato took me to the stable, which had a small light inside. There was Sandro in one stall, another horse in a stall next to him. Sandro was eating, and I was shown where he usually slept. That was comforting but, mostly, it was surprising to me that the Italians seemed concerned that the opinion of an English POW actually mattered. Perhaps we all forgot war for a while and behaved as if we were human beings.

Except for such rarities, this general work routine continued for months. We didn't work on Sundays, which was nice. It was like another prison camp on Sundays because we had to stay confined all day. But on those days, since there was no work, the girls either went to their homes a few miles away or stayed around and came out by our camp. We were a novelty to them, different, foreign. But no one actually struck up a romance. Words, only. We couldn't do it.

Camp Life

We prisoners naturally got closer as the time went on. We became friends. We knew we were strangers who were forced together, but we got to know each other and care for each other. Even the cook changed. He realized he'd been silly. He finally got to give up being a cook, though, which helped his attitude. The Sergeant-Major didn't like the way he'd been. He thought that was a shame. "You all have enough to put up with without that," he said once.

Later the Sergeant-Major asked me how things were going after the cook was re-assigned, and I told him it was all right. And it was. We never really got another cook. The Sergeant-Major arranged for us to switch off. He put the former cook in my squad. I thought, Who needs this? But the fellow put himself out to make it work. He was okay and everything turned out all right.

We worked each day until around five-thirty or six. The guards were there all the time, of course. We were never supposed to communicate with the civilians, but that was ridiculous and, after a while, we spoke quite a bit, considering the language problems. The rice fields were large, and we were all spread out across them. If one of us had made a break for it, he may well have made it. The guards really couldn't keep too close an eye on us all.

One of the guards was older than the rest, and he was usually tired. Clearly he didn't want to be there. I used to tease him, ask him if he'd let me see his gun, talk about the girls, just try to take the mickey out of him. It was my way of having fun, I suppose. One time he was lying back against a tree and I actually did pick up his gun, but all he said was, "No, Carlos, no." I put it back down. I used to tease him that if he didn't behave, I'd escape. He hated that. It wouldn't look good for him if someone escaped on his watch. But the guards were generally good to us, quite fair. Of course they always had to keep in mind that the Allies might win the war, and if that happened, they could be punished. So they were in a strange position, one they didn't really want to be in at all.

It's a British soldier's duty to attempt to escape: Make everything difficult and try to escape, that's what we're told. But we were pretty cautious, plus I confess we didn't have it so bad that we wanted to rock the boat too much. Besides, we needed to find out more about where we were, and we were told of several Germans in the area at some military training camp. Another rumour, perhaps, but we couldn't know for sure. We talked about escape often, and most of the fellows thought we wouldn't be wise to do it. We felt we were just lucky to be where we were. If one of us had tried, that would have been the end of what we considered to be a reasonable life for the rest of us. I think everyone knew that and wouldn't attempt it until it looked like we could all make it out.

We'd all been in the camp in Africa. That's how we ended up in Italy. If we'd been captured in France, we'd have gone to Germany.

But being in Africa, we went to Italy. There were a lot of British and South Africans and New Zealanders captured out in the Mediterranean or the Middle East or Africa. They all went to Italy. The guys there seemed to realize that to do what you were supposed to do—escape— would have been a real crime, not only against yourself but also against your fellow prisoners. We really didn't know how to get home from there, either. That was a big part of the problem. We didn't know how to go about getting to Switzerland at that time. We just didn't know. It wasn't as though we had experienced men among us who could advise us, and we had no maps.

We understood that the Swiss were on the side of the Allies even though they were supposed to be neutral. I learned about this from a chap I went to school with who ended up at that same camp in Africa. He walked up to me one day at that camp and sort of stood in front of me, looking kind of quizzically. I noticed him, but I just ignored him. I didn't recognize him. Finally he looked right into my eyes and said, "Charlie?" I shook my head, couldn't believe it. I said, "Alex?" I could hardly comprehend that this was the same guy I knew. He'd recognized me right away, though. Of course he told me all about his experience being captured, becoming a prisoner. He'd had a bad time, worse than I. He also filled me in about the various positions of the countries, European and North American, tried to let me know who to trust and how things stood. Of course he was going largely on rumours too, but at least his were a bit fresher than mine. He'd been captured a few months later than I had.

Italy was losing its country to the Germans, no doubt about that, and I learned from the farmers that there were many fascists in the area who were friends of the Germans. They were often the ones who were simply afraid that Italy would lose, and they wanted to be on good terms with the victors. But we knew we had to be careful of them. They dressed as civilians, and we couldn't tell who was who. Who could we trust?

We often talked in the evenings about making a break for Switzerland, and we tried to put together a plan for this. Every chance we got, we started collecting civilian clothes and any other provisions we felt we might need. An old hat here, a backpack there. Anything that might seem helpful. Even a pair of shoelaces might come in handy. Since we had things pretty good where we were, we could take our time with the plans. We weren't desperate. That made a big difference. One evening the Sergeant-Major told me to sit down and, in a roundabout way, he let me know me that Italy was in bad trouble and he wouldn't be surprised if they quit the war. He went on to say that some morning we might get up and find that the guards had left. Naturally I told my mates of the situation, told them what the Sergeant-Major had told me; but of course we didn't know when it would happen, or even if it would happen.

A Change

It happened, though, and much sooner than we'd expected. One morning I woke up before the others and walked outside into the yard and I didn't see any guards. No one. I was stunned, thought I was dreaming, even though I'd been forewarned. I immediately went to the gate and checked it. It was unlocked. I opened it and walked right out, just as though I lived there as a free man. That is a moment I'll never forget. Never. Just walked out. I stood there a minute and took a deep breath. Unbelievable. My first breath as a free man for nearly two years. I proceeded right to the office of the Sergeant-Major, and it was also unlocked. Of course, all the important materials were gone and the office was basically empty, but that meant nothing to me. That's not what I was after. I just stood there and looked around, my heart beating hard enough for me to feel it, my hands sweating.

I dashed back into the house and told the fellows it was over, that Italy had dropped out. I suggested that we have breakfast and talk about it all. The guys started whooping and hollering, just like England had won the bloody World Cup. They raced outside and out the gate. Smiles, claps on the back, all the usual. It was wonderful. Of course we weren't home yet, but we sure as hell felt a lot closer to home than we had the day before. So we sat down and kicked our options around: What to do next? How to do it? How to get home? We finally decided we'd be wisest to stay in the woods, at least for a while, and not to try to get away on our own. I was to get word to Mintin, a journalist who'd shown up occasionally around there and, as we understood, worked with the Italian Underground. We knew it was likely that the Germans would go to the prison camps and move the prisoners to Germany, or kill them. Certainly the Germans weren't about to let us walk away. We had no do doubt about that.

We knew the Germans would fight to the death. We hadn't expected that the Italians would leave the war and we'd have no Germans ready to take over. We'd heard from the farmers that the Allies were getting closer to us, that they had been advancing into northern Italy. One rumour had them as far as Rome by that time, only a couple hundred miles away. One of the farmers had told me about it. I told the guys it was up to each of them as to what to do, but that I thought we should stay around. My opinion was that we should go to work, as usual, then try to get organized, to go off in groups and make plans.

Within a couple weeks, the first German soldiers showed up in the village of Monticello. We were there, of course, working in the fields and sleeping in the forest. The Germans apparently asked the farmers where the prisoners were and the Italians played dumb, didn't say anything about us, said we'd just disappeared. The foreman of our group, Guiseppi, told me all about the Germans having come. The farmers had put themselves and their families at great risk to help us, and I shall never forget that. Guiseppi also told me Mintin had organized the Resistance in the area and, when any Germans approached the village, some young Italian men on bicycles would rush out to the fields and let us know we needed to hide.

We were concerned that the Germans—or the fascistic Italians— might come to the house where we'd been held prisoner, so we all went to the farms we'd been working for. The farmers became our employers, now, instead of our overseers. We worked as farm laborers. This didn't last, though. The good times were gone because of the constant fear, ours and the Italians'. The Italians had to look out for their families, of course. We swore among ourselves that we would never let the Italians down, never do any thing that might jeopardize them. We had to make ourselves scarce. We slept out in the woods. We were never together as an entire group. In fact, after that first day without the guards, I had very little communication with any of the others except for the four in our group. I never saw the others, for the most part. I'd get together once in a while to talk with four or five. others, but never all of them.

Two rules: Think about escaping, and think about helping the Italian families. We'd heard—rumours again—that families in other villages had been shot by German troops for helping the prisoners-of-war, so we stood strong in our resolve to keep our "employers" safe. Of course that meant we were constantly watching out not only for ourselves but also for the Italians. I never felt I had the authority to order any of the men to do anything, but no one tried to escape. We talked about it all the time, but I always encouraged them to be smart if they decided to go, to contact the Resistance. You had to get through the Italian Alps in order to get away, and that wasn't easy. A person couldn't do it in thin clothes. You'd be dead. This was late autumn and it was cold in the mountains. I finally got in touch with the Resistance, through Mintin. He came to us to tell us what was going on in the war. I told him some of the fellows wanted to make a go for it and he agreed to help.

Leaving Italy

Mintin arranged for two men and a woman to come to the village. They were well-dressed and looked very professional. They couldn't speak English, but they let us know that we couldn't stay where we were, that it was too dangerous for everyone, including the Italians. They'd put together a plan to help us get out, two or three of us a week. Since I was NCO, I would be in the last group to go.

We soon learned the others were getting out because the farmers would tell us. Sometimes we'd connect with someone from another crew and get a more specific report, in English. The Underground was a well-organized system, and they would help us get out of Italy without raising alarms. Our men were leaving every five to seven days, two or three at a time. I knew my time was getting close, but that didn't mean I wasn't nervous. I didn't know when the Germans might come up to Monticello again, for one thing. Or if a couple of our men got captured, who could predict what might occur? That could alert a heavy manhunt in the area, jeopardizing not only the prisoners but also the farmers.

My day finally came, though, a month or so after the first of the fellows left. By that time only three of us were still there. Late in the afternoon, Mintin showed up in the field where I was working. He was with one of the farmers from the town. I knew they had either good news— I was leaving—or bad news—our men had been captured. They brought good news. They told me the rest of us were to leave the next morning. The Germans, they told us, were getting very close and we had to move fast. They said one of the farmers was a fascist and they were all worried about him. They told us to be in a small shop in Bena, a vineyard in nearby Novarra, early the next morning. Someone from the Resistance would meet us there. That's all they told us. "The less you know the less you can tell," they said. That made sense.

The next morning we made our way to Bena, looking as little like Englishmen as possible—we tried to look like Italians. I wore a hat since I was fair-haired and the hat covered my hair. The other two blokes were taller than average Italians, so they walked bent over. We met the Underground guides in the shop, as planned, and we went on into the back. They had some civilian clothes for us and we tried our best to fit into them. Old clothes, but that's how it should be. I had dark trousers and a dark jacket. They didn't match, and they were way too big for me, but that was fine with me. I was also given a small attaché case, like you'd take to work. It was full of rice. I was supposed to look like a clerk of some kind.

We were then told to meet back in the square and to hang around as though we were bored. Before long, a farmer came along on a horse and cart with a huge wine barrel. Huge. He pulled into a farmer's yard just off the square, and signaled to us to wander back there. We had to be casual so no one would suspect us. So we meandered into the back part of this old farmhouse and into the area where this horse and cart had ended up. The driver told us to climb into the wine barrel. I thought it was a joke, a silly mystery, but it wasn't. That was the plan.

All three of us squeezed in. The smell was horrendous. I swear we were all drunk from fumes by the time we got out. The driver didn't speak English and didn't understand my Italian. He wouldn't say where we were going, or I didn't understand. He went past everyone in town, though, just drove that cart right through the village, and of course almost everyone we passed must have known what was going on. How could you keep something like that a secret in such a small village. It was unbelievable. Like a cheap spy novel. A joke.

We were in that barrel for about an hour, *clop-clop-clop-clop*. We kept hearing those horse's hooves on the cobblestones or on the dirt paths. Nearly pitch black inside, of course, except for some very slight cracks where little streams of light could come through. Then, suddenly, the noise of the hooves on the road changed, turned into more of a clickety sound. *Click-clack, click-clack*. We knew we were somewhere else, but we didn't know where. We couldn't see out. And we had to be very quiet. "*Silencio!*" the driver would say. We knew we'd gone onto another cobblestoned road.

The farmer took us to a part of a brewer's yard where no one could see anything. It was something like going into a garage. Someone opened the trap door to the wine barrel, and we all rolled out. The fumes were really something. We staggered to our feet and were really glad to be in the fresh air again. People stood all around us, Resistance people. They shook our hands—they shake hands every five minutes in Italy—and they told us where we were. Then they told us a woman would be there shortly to let us know what we'd be doing next. So we were taken into the farmer's house and given some coffee and something to eat. That was the first food we'd had all day.

Soon a very attractive woman of about thirty or thirty-five came along, quite classy. I had no idea who she was or what she was going to do, but she was with the Resistance. The idea was that we'd follow her—sounds like an old movie, doesn't it?—she'd walk along the pavement and we'd follow her about fifty yards distant. Of course we couldn't all walk along together or we'd be spotted in a minute, so I walked on one side of the street—the same side as the woman—and the other two walked on the opposite side. I was a bit worried about my mates. I knew I could walk like an Italian civilian but the other two, well, I'd seen them walk before, and they always walked like soldiers. Some people who get used to walking in military fashion find it difficult to walk otherwise. It's in their arms. I tried to teach these two blokes, intelligent men, to walk more naturally. I'd say, "Walk like an out-of-work Italian," and they just couldn't. And I stopped them. I said, "For crissakes, you bastards, act like a beggar in the street. You've got nothing. *Nothing*. You're a drunk. Walk like that." That seemed to help a bit.

They'd start out fine, but each time after a half dozen steps, one or the other would start swinging his arms about. So we practiced it half a dozen times or more. It was hard for them to relax.

When we actually got to the street, then, we had to keep those two apart since once they got together they'd start swinging their arms like they were marching. The Germans weren't likely to spot it, in my opinion, but the Italian Resistance fighters were worried that we'd be spotted, so that was it. We took off. We walked around a corner and down a street, quite a long way. I was nervous as hell because I saw a lot of Germans sitting along the walls and riding in vehicles. They weren't out looking for us, of course, but they were all there, everywhere we looked. They seemed to me to be wicked and angry, everything I'd most feared they would be. So of course I had to act cool, had to convince them that I wasn't as frightened as I was.

I followed the woman, and she did her part well. She was very smart. Her only trouble would have been if a German had approached her, which could have happened since she was so good looking. She could have been harassed for any number of reasons, even just because a German soldier wanted to make time with a good-looking woman and wanted to show off to his mates. But it didn't occur, thank God.

I was behind her, maybe twenty or thirty yards, and the other two were across the street, looking just like a couple of British soldiers, as far as I could tell, and I wasn't sure what to do. I thought I'd have to cross the road and bump into them to make them stop marching. It worked all right, though. That old brown derby I was wearing to cover up my hair was too big for me, and it drooped down around my ears, but I suppose that just made me look more like a strange little Italian man out for some business.

At one point, I had to follow our leader around a corner. I didn't know what I'd find, of course, since I'd never been to this city before. And the other blokes would have to follow me. Just as I turned the corner, a large group of Germans was right in front of me getting out of a truck. Ten feet away. Close. Real close. They were running into a house right next to me and seemed to be after someone who might be in the house. If I'd been another yard closer, they'd have knocked me over. The Germans wouldn't have cared, though. Italians were nothing to them, especially now that the Italians had got out of the war. The Germans hated them. But fortunately they didn't hit me. They walked right in front of me as if I wasn't even there. But I was more than a bit tense. I had to pause while they raced past me. I wanted to kill them. I hated the Germans. Of course I couldn't have killed anything, not in my condition. So I just stood there and let them by. My mates had turned the corner too, by that time, and they were walking like soldiers again. They looked to me as though they were preparing for an attack.

All I did was think, over and over, *I'm an Italian, I'm an Italian.*

There was nothing else for me to do. Heavy suitcase. Scum of the earth. Germans all around me. I had to be *nothing*. I looked again for the woman, who'd kept walking, of course, and I caught sight of her just as she'd turned into an office building. Fortunately the others saw her go in, too, so we all followed her. She never spoke a word, just looked over at the elevator. And we all got in. We went up a few floors and got out into a corridor. She walked over to the first office, opened the door, turned and smiled. Then she said, in perfect English, "Come in, please." She spoke English!

Inside were a half dozen Italian Resistance men, all smiles. "Come in," they said. They had wine, food. We were awestruck. Truly. I said to my blokes, "Let's see what they've got to say." What else could we do? The Italian woman spoke with the men in Italian, planning the next move.

Mintin was among them. He explained to us that the next day we'd be following this same woman to the railway station. We were told not to approach the woman, nor to speak to anybody if we could help it, nor to recognize anybody. Just to hang around waiting for the train. She would buy the tickets and get them to us.

Then they put us up for the night, had real beds for us and some wine to calm us down. We were all very tense. We talked long into the night, all of us much too excited to sleep very well. It felt like we were in the middle of a novel. All I could do was fantasize about freedom, about escaping from this country and arriving in Switzerland. After so many months and so many deprivations, it finally seemed that it might end.

The next day we got different clothes—warmer, for going to the mountains—and had a bit of breakfast and some strong coffee. Mintin explained to us that we'd be met at the last stop on the railway. We were to get off the train and turn to our right, then walk about half a mile along the tracks. At about that point, we were to listen for a man's call to us. That was the man who was to get us over the mountains and into Switzerland. The Resistance men also gave me a letter to present to the British Consulate in Switzerland explaining that if the British wanted the Italians to help more, they'd have to provide guns and food. This was, obviously, an important letter, and I took the assignment seriously. The Resistance people I met were smart, efficient, and knew what it was all about. The Resistance Movement had started long before the Italians had left the war and these people had had experience in this.

We got to the station in the early afternoon. I'm convinced that I saw other Englishmen there, no doubt in my mind. One guy was holding a newspaper upside down. He must have been terrified. I don't know how he got away with it. He must have just been too nervous to even notice. Fortunately, or maybe unfortunately, it was an extremely busy day at the station. Troop movements were in full force, mostly all German. Lots of traffic. The station was packed, no place even to sit down. Everyone was there to get the train, but no one knew when the trains would arrive during the war. How could they? It was a mess. Germans were everywhere, but none of them seemed at all interested in anything. They seemed bored, in fact. I learned later that most of the Germans at the station were on their way home, either for leave or because of being wounded. That helped explain things.

The woman had bought the tickets, along with a newspaper, and as she passed by me, she handed me the paper with the tickets tucked inside. She was marvelous. Very quiet. As the train arrived, she gave me a bit of a kiss, like I was her boyfriend, and the three of us got on the train. It seemed as though everyone in the station wanted on that train. Fortunately there were so many of us that nobody worried much about three strange-looking Italians. What I learned later was that the Germans were most concerned with Italian soldiers who were escaping. Not British prisoners. So we were lucky in that respect. I'm not sure why they didn't suspect us of being Italian soldiers on the run, though, but they didn't seem to. Probably we were too beaten down looking after so much time as prisoners.

We'd been told to try to get on a railway car with no Germans aboard. That turned out to be ridiculous, though, since the Germans took over every car. We finally spotted some seats opposite two Italian elderly men. They were sitting there talking to each other. I didn't want to sit near them because I didn't want them to talk with me. But it would have been silly not to sit there. That would have been too obvious. So I just sat there along with one of the other guys I'd escaped with. The Italians, of course, are great for making conversation and I certainly didn't want to talk. So that made me nervous. I don't know why, though, but they didn't try to talk to us. I tried to make it clear in my body language that I didn't want to talk. If they'd spoken to us and we'd responded and they'd figured it out, they might well have been fascists and turned us in. Two Germans were standing in the aisle right next to me, and they looked about ten feet tall. If we hadn't had experience as prisoners, lots of practice trying to deceive the guards, we might not have got away with it. If I'd been closer to my training as a soldier, I'm sure I'd have acted differently. But it worked. We made it.

We couldn't get off fast enough when we finally came to the last stop. It was pitch black when we stepped out of the train. Others got off there, too. It must have been about midnight by this time. We turned right and walked along the road by the track. They'd told us about how long it would take, but that was all. It was pitch black, so we couldn't see a thing, and it was getting colder and colder. Finally I heard a voice saying something in Italian. I said, "I'm English," in Italian. A man came out from nowhere. He had a tiny torch. He smiled and he asked us, in Italian, "Are you going to Monticule?" Monticule was a Swiss village. That was our signal.

It worked. I don't know how or why, but it did. I asked if we could sit down a minute and he said, "No. They're everywhere." He was an official Italian guide for the mountains. He said, "All you are to do is follow me. No speaking. No rest."

We could barely see him and he moved fast, but we kept up. We hiked for three or four hours. Every so often we could see some lights in the distance going on and off, flashing, and we knew these were the lights of the Germans. That reminded us to keep quiet and to move carefully.

We walked on, mostly up steep mountainsides, and I felt ever more tired and cold. Snow covered everything but the trail. If I hadn't been so motivated, I don't know how I'd have kept going. We hadn't eaten much all day and we'd all been too nervous to sleep either the night before or during the train ride. But we were all definitely motivated.

We only saw one other person that night, an old man with a huge dog. He passed us going the other way about two hours after we'd started. We saw him and he saw us. No questions whatever, though, and no greeting. We just passed each other and stared.

At first light, we got to someplace which felt like the side of a mountain but was probably just a steep hill. We'd been told that we would eventually, in early morning, see Switzerland. It was about five o'clock by then, and we could see it, all of us. There was no light ban there as there had been in Italy. We could see streets, buildings. It looked like heaven. Even now, years later, when I think of a paradise, I picture that first view of Switzerland after all those months of captivity.

The first time I saw it we weren't but a couple hundred yards away. I couldn't believe it. But I also saw the wire, barbed wire. And a small lake just in front of the wire. This was border wire, and alongside it was a border guard. The Italians would be on the side we were on—they chose fascists for these positions—and the Swiss would be on the other side. Our guide told us we'd have to hide in the bush for the right time to cross over. We'd have no trouble with the Swiss authorities, but getting by the Italian guards, that was the problem. Although it was still fairly dark, we could be seen. We were a bit too late. We had to find a good place to lie down until evening, until the guard changed. We were so close, but we couldn't go, so we just lay there in the bushes, in a copse. Slept, lazed. Waited. It was horrible.

Re-Capture

Suddenly we heard voices, German voices. I thought—hoped—they were German-speaking Swiss, but I was dreaming. They were a ways off, but we could tell they were getting near. I didn't see how they could spot us since we were all completely surrounded by trees and underbrush. They got closer, though, and we all held our breath. We could hear their footsteps. I began to sweat, started thinking about that letter the Italian Resistance had entrusted me with, wondered what I'd do with it if I got caught.

We probably only had about five minutes from when we first heard their voices until we saw their boots through the bushes, but I swear it lasted for hours. I was afraid and angry and depressed and a bit insane, all at once. I couldn't believe it was happening again. Impossible. Just when we seemed to be free, just when we were so close we could practically reach out and touch the Swiss countryside.

I don't know to this day how they found us, but there they were. They suddenly encircled us. This was still early in the morning, maybe seven or eight. I think the old man with the dog turned us in, the man we'd passed on the trail earlier that morning. We later learned that they'd thought we were Italian soldiers trying to escape the country. The Germans considered such men to be deserters, traitors. They didn't treat them at all well.

As soon as I realized what was happening, I feared they'd kill our guide. They would have, too, I'm sure. I didn't think they could have much of an idea how many of us were there, so as I was getting out of the thicket, I leaned over to the guide and whispered to him, in my best Italian, "You've got to hide, stay here, don't go out." And he did. The rest of us came out and created a scene, raised a ruckus. We tried to divert the Germans' attention. And the guide slithered away deeper into the underbrush on his belly. He actually escaped. They couldn't see us well enough to know someone else was with us.

They marched us single file right next to the border—we could have reached out and touched the barbed wire—for a couple of hours, probably four miles. I became petrified with fear that they'd find the letter I'd been asked to deliver, and I knew I had to get rid of it somehow. Where could I throw it, though, so it wouldn't be picked up later, during the day? So while it was still dark, I faked a coughing spell and stuffed the letter into my mouth. Then as we continued to march I just chewed and chewed until I was able to swallow it.

By the time they stopped us it was daylight. Around nine, I'd say. We passed German camps and German patrols every few miles. They were everywhere. The ones who captured us still seemed to think we were Italians. They hadn't asked to see our papers. They just thought we were a bunch of Italians trying to get out of the war and they never spoke to us.

They took us to a big old building near a mountain village and brought us to an officer, a real ranting and raving maniac. We didn't have any idea what he was shouting about, but he was clearly crazed. He was the kind of man I fear most because I had no idea what he might do next. This was my first real experience with Germans since I'd been captured in North Africa. I'd seen them several times, but I hadn't actually interacted with them, if you could call this an interaction. Mostly we just listened while this madman raved on. We'd had visions of Germans, of course, from the stories we'd heard, but we hadn't seen much of them. This guy fit the stereotype.

The Firing Squad

Just as I was thinking he was softening, things got crazy again. This officer started shouting at us and then at his men, shouting and spitting and waving his hands. I don't know what had set him off, but I think someone said something to him about us which caused him to fly off the handle. The next thing we knew, three guards grabbed us and spun us around and practically dragged us out of his office into a courtyard. The guards shouted at us and pushed us up a wall of one of the outbuildings, and they ordered us to put our hands up above our heads. Then they stepped back and drew their weapons, waiting, apparently, for the command from this crazy officer. We said to each other, "Well, this is it."

We were ready to accept the fact that we were going to be shot as we stood there like idiots. I can remember that moment perfectly, exactly where I was and exactly how it all looked and smelled. It seemed, even at the time, to be absurd, but this was the kind of action we'd come to expect from the Germans from all the stories we'd heard, so I really wasn't surprised that it was happening. In fact, a strange sort of peace passed through me as I stood there. Not panic, but peace. He continued to scream at one person or another, and then at us for trying to escape, for being traitors and Italian deserters. Suddenly it hit me. *He didn't know we were British.* Since I had my identity tag on, I just turned to the officer and held it out and said, loudly, in English, with an attitude: "Stop this! We're British soldiers! We're not Italians! You can't do this!"

He went bananas. He yelled and screamed and hollered and waved and then yelled and screamed some more. But he didn't give the order to fire. He just shouted and stormed off, back to his office, leaving us with the guards, their pistols in their hands. I think that saved our lives. I can't swear to it, of course, and I really don't know why I did it, but I had to do something. And I had nothing to lose at that point since he was planning to shoot us anyway. He was such an offensive bastard. Shouting about how he could kill us all. Well, Germany was on its way out and I believe he knew that, too.

Everything changed after that. The officer returned and shouted at his men to get us out of there, and they marched us off to Como, the town near the lake. They just marched us along the street. There were six or eight of us, by now, all English. Where the others came from I'll never know. I hadn't seen them before. We marched across fields and hills and then, suddenly, into this city, Como.

Transported Again

The guards stopped us on one of the streets and, as we stood on the corner, a tram came along and the guards stopped it. They then herded us aboard. It was unbelievable. First, of course, they forced all the regular passengers to get off. Then they put us aboard. The conductor came around with a box for the fare, just as though we were regular passengers. And we were bloody prisoners! In a war! It was like a joke. And the guards paid the conductor. I saw it but I still can't believe it.

When we got off a few minutes later, we were near a military barracks. That's where they had us stop. There were lots of Italians there, of course, and they were told we were escaped English prisoners. The Germans shouted some more, and then they put us in with the Italian prisoners. That's where we stayed for the next several days.

On the second day in the cells, an Italian cook approached us and tried to strike up a conversation. He loved the English, he said, and wanted to help us. He spoke a little broken English, and he told us he had weapons and could help us. I didn't trust him, and I warned everyone to leave him alone. I could see right through him. "Don't touch any of that," I told the others. He was a nasty piece of work, a fascist. I hated him. I told him to get stuffed! Later I saw him in a car with some Germans. Bad news. You always had to watch out for such men.

We were at this barracks for a week or ten days. Finally, they brought in a big truck, open in the back, and they forced us to get in. Four German guards stood there with their rifles pointed at us. Italians pushed us on the truck, but German guards manned the truck, all with rifles. The use of rifles was silly, really, since pistols would have been better, but that's the way they had it. Maybe they didn't have pistols. I don't know. One of the Germans told us we'd be heading through Brenner Pass to Germany where we'd be held. There were about twenty of us in the truck, something like that.

I felt that the longer we were on the truck the worse off we'd be. From the rumours I'd heard, we'd be in horrible shape if we got taken to Germany. I wasn't far from the back, so I suggested to a couple other prisoners that we should make a go for it, try to overpower the guards and escape. One of the guys said we couldn't all make it. Some would get killed. As far as I was concerned, I didn't want to see anybody get hurt, but I was so frustrated that I felt I had to make a go of it. Still, I knew he was right, that everyone wouldn't make it, most likely. I was getting frantic, though, and starting to panic.

When you get into a situation like that, you think funny things. I thought of my parents, of how they'd take it if I got killed. I had a sense that it was now or never to escape, but I just didn't feel I could do that to my parents. I felt guilty that I was a prisoner at all, as though I'd done something wrong. And then to get myself killed seemed really wrong. Of course everything gets all mixed up while you're in the middle of it all.

I finally agreed this wasn't the time. We didn't know what was in store for us when we got where we were going, but we decided we'd be better off waiting and seeing. I knew something about Brenner Pass, that it was a huge pass through the mountains that was made before the war. I figured that they'd take us via train, and I didn't like that, either. I'd heard rumours—rumours again—about how the prisoners had been transported by train and had ended up dying in a freezing boxcar. I truly feared such a journey.

The truck stopped at a railway siding and we were herded onto a cattle car. It wasn't a passenger train, of course, like the ones we'd ridden in Italy. This was nothing but a bloody freight train. There were dozens of others on this train who had been picked up from various places, maybe over a hundred. Allied soldiers, including Italians. We were going to be taken somewhere, but no one seemed to know for sure where. The first stop, though, would most likely be Austria.

Innsbruck

I didn't know the geography well, but I felt—wrongly—that Innsbruck wasn't far from where we were, and I thought that's where we'd be going. It was getting late in the year, around Christmas time, and there was lots of snow. So we rode in a cattle car with several of the guards hanging on the side of the train. Lots of Italian ex-soldiers were pushed into the car as well. The car was only half full, though, not too bad. At least you could sit down. They slammed the door on us and everything went black. Couldn't see a thing. We seemed to travel forever, days and nights. You lose track of time when it's dark all the time, and how could you tell how long you're there?

We finally did get to Innsbruck, but the trip had taken longer than I'd expected. We were all told to get off, the whole trainload, quite a long train. The English-speaking prisoners were herded into a transfer camp, if you want to call it that. It appeared to be empty when we arrived, but the trainload of prisoners filled it up pretty quickly. And once we got to know our way around the camp, we discovered that it already held hundreds of Allied prisoners and that some of them seemed to have been there for quite a while. I never found out what that was all about, whether they were there permanently or what was going on. But they stayed on after we left.

We remained in this camp for a week or so. It was a madhouse. No control. Guards everywhere, snow, barbed wire, lots of muck and mud, no blankets. The guards pushed us into a room and left us to make the best of it. We just slept on the wet floor, curled up in our coats, if we were lucky enough to have one. They gave us some food, some bread and water, but they didn't distribute it. They just threw it on the floor of our room and we had to fend for ourselves.

One day while I was at this camp I heard someone say, "They're showing a film!" "Where?" "Around the corner." It was crazy. No organization at all. Just a madhouse. We saw all sorts of people going toward a building where they were apparently presenting a film. I don't remember the name of it now, but there it was. An American film! I never really saw much of it, to tell the truth. I just couldn't stay awake. But I went, of course. It was some kind of relief, and we were all hungry for any kind of relief. Amazing. Poor food. No water. And a bloody movie! And who showed the movie? Was it one of them or one of us? This was a crazy war.

Finally they ordered us out of this camp and marched us to Innsbruck Railway Station and put us on another railway car, another cattle car. This time we were absolutely crammed in. This time we couldn't sit down. We were pushed in by the guards who used their bayonets to prod us. They must have emptied the camp that day and put everyone into these cars.

They slammed the doors and locked them. They didn't place any guards inside, of course. Why would they? And the train pulled out. We didn't know where we were going, couldn't see anything, but also couldn't relax. We could hardly even breathe, in fact. Lots of men started moaning out of sickness. Several of the men in our car were sick. The Germans didn't care. They treated us like animals, but I still think of them as the animals. They allowed us no water, no food, no toilet facilities. It was awful. No one could sit down since it was so crowded. We all stood pressed in against one another. After a while your legs feel numb, like they're not even there. You couldn't do any-thing, couldn't even bend over to scratch your leg. Certainly couldn't empty your bowels. If you had to go to the toilet, after a while you just had to let it go while you were standing there. You can imagine what it must have smelled like after a couple days. It was miserable, truly miserable. The only opening was a small aperture near the roof to provide some air.

We were in this hell hole of a railway car for about a week. A week of horror. They only opened the door one time, but no one could get out, even to go to the latrine. I didn't know where we were, of course, except that we were going from Innsbruck into Germany. We were told nothing. They didn't want us to know anything. That's part of their technique to break you, part of their torture. If someone would ever ask a guard a question, he might say something, but not much. The guards only spoke in German anyway, so no one understood whatever they might have said.

All those movies about people hollering out to offer encourage-ment? Just movies. You know the lines: "Keep your chin up, fellows, stiff upper lip," that sort of thing? Never happened on this train, anyway. I'm not saying it never happened, but it didn't happen with us. People were too miserable, and any such encouragement probably would have been met with jeers, or just nothing. You just didn't want to hear it.

Unfortunately, your mind is not upbeat or positive in such situations. My only feeling was they're not going to get me. Others felt that way, too, I know. We talked about that. "We'll get you someday, you bastards." That was it. "We'll get you in the end." We had nothing, nothing. Actually we Brits have a good sense of humor under most circumstances, I think. About all we ever talked about, even aboard the train, was what we'd do when we got home, about food, about our girls. Just what was in the future. Hope. That's what it was all about, and that's what seemed to keep us going.

All we really wanted to do was stay alive. We'd keep thinking about the end of the war, about eating, and about women. You couldn't just moan and groan. You were hungry and cold, but you couldn't think about all that. You just had to keep talking with others and try to keep your spirits up. Ironically, it was only because of all the people that we survived, I'm certain. It was freezing, but the body temperatures of the prisoners, all jammed up against each other, kept us from freezing to death. It was a wicked, nasty way to treat people, but we hadn't seen anything yet. We couldn't believe people treated others that way, but we didn't really know the Germans. Not yet.

Arrival in Germany

We arrived someplace in the country in Germany, but we didn't know where. The train stopped and we could hear the guards talking and shouting, but no one opened the door to our car. We stayed stationery for a long while, hours. Finally we started banging on the inside of the car. "Let us out! Let us out!" That went on for more hours. I don't know what their game was. We were cold and people were sick, and we needed some fresh air.

Finally the guards opened the door and the sunlight hit us, blinded us. We'd been riding for several days, at least four days. Not one of us could stand up properly on our own. Our legs just wouldn't work. The guards were all around us with their guns pointed at us, as if any of us had the strength to try to make a run for it. But they didn't let us out. They just opened the door and left us standing there with that sun glaring at us. It was absurd, once again.

One officer who could speak a little English finally approached our car. He told us that the compound—if you could call it that, actually a branch of a larger camp, a cage for all of Germany's enemies: Russians, French, and so on—the compound wasn't ready yet. He said we'd have to wait in the car until it was ready. And they slammed the door shut again. This is the truth. They closed the bloody doors on us one more time, forced us back into the boxcar. Ridiculous. We never saw anything, never saw a building. Just countryside, trees, snow. "The compound isn't ready," he said. The compound wasn't ready. Amazing.

While the door was open, we asked for food and drink, but they gave us nothing. I was standing on the side in the middle towards the door. I wasn't the only NCO this time, and I certainly wasn't in charge. We had sergeants and sergeant-majors and even some officers among us. Everyone protested and shouted, and they finally gave us some water. I don't remember if anyone among us spoke German, but I don't think they did. I can't describe how miserable we were. What we had was a boxcar full of human beings and every one of them was hurting for one reason or another. It was like we got to our lowest levels at last. Nobody cared about us. We were completely on our own. You feel desolate and lonely and you know you're not wanted by these people. You're just in the way. You don't even think about how they shouldn't do this to you. Instead you're thinking, Cristomighty, when are they going to behave like human beings?

But you know they're not going to behave like human beings or they'd have done it days ago. Maybe the soldier in charge had no choice. Or maybe he just didn't like us. Who can say? It was inhuman. All you think about at that point is getting out. Anywhere. You're not sane at all. In fact, you don't care about anything but surviving. I remember thinking about how I could get away and get my own back, get a taste of revenge against these creatures, overpower a guard and steal his weapon. I wasn't thinking rationally. You're not saying, Okay, I'll do it this way and that way and escape and get food and so on. No brains. Just surviving and hating.

It was the next evening—seems a long time—when finally the officers and soldiers came around and opened the boxcars, all of them. The car I was in was somewhere in the middle of the convoy. It was a long train. Some cars had goods in them of one kind or another, but most had prisoners, or at least that's what I observed. I wasn't looking too carefully at what was going on, wasn't keeping a bloody diary. I was only interested in getting out and getting food so I could sleep.

Thinking back, I believe it was actually worse in the boat in the Mediterranean than it was in the train. The boat was scarier, at least for me. I don't think I believed I was going to die while I was on the train, but I did think that aboard that boat. While I was in the boxcar, I felt that many men wouldn't survive the train journey, but I was sure I could make it. I never thought the Germans were out to kill us. They just seemed to me to want to show they were superior.

But on the boat, down in the hold, it was totally black, complete darkness, and many of the men were seasick, and we could often hear the planes overhead firing at us. We were all terribly frightened aboard that boat. Men were moaning and praying. People used any excuse to get out and go to the toilet. And just the idea of being on board a ship—water all around us—was rather frightening.

At least on the train you felt you had some chance to get off. You didn't have the feeling that the train was going to be blasted away. But on the ship, if that went, you were gone. The idea of our own British airplanes shelling the ship was horrible.

At least half the men on the train couldn't walk when we finally got out of the boxcar. No one got down easily and the Germans didn't help matters. "Come on, come on," they'd shout, in German. "*Aus! Aus!*" Some men had dysentery and all kinds of problems, and they were taken away. But you really only thought about yourself at that time, about surviving. Much as you didn't enjoy seeing others taken away, you were still looking for the food bowl. Where am I? What am I going to do? How long will I be here? What will I eat? When will I eat?

4

GERMANY

THERE WERE A LOT OF PRISONERS AT THE CAMP ALREADY, HUNDREDS.
The Germans separated us according to nationality, and I couldn't tell
what the other men's nationalities were. I know there were lots besides
British, though. They ordered us to walk to the outside of the outer
cage, a huge area surrounded by barbed wire fencing, which of course
we did. We were stopped by the fence, though, and we were able to
look into the inner cage. We could see hundreds of other prisoners
crammed into the cage. Some were dressed as soldiers, but others
appeared to be civilians. So many prisoners. I guessed that they were
Czechs, Poles, and French, but who knows? We weren't told anything
about where we'd be going or what was next for us. We all just stood
there and waited, watching the men in the inner cage.

Finally, after the guards and officers shouted at us, we got up and
moved out, marched to the entrance of a brand new compound. Then
they told us to stand there and wait. They told the senior NCOs to step
forward, and I stayed where I was. I wouldn't be senior at this camp
as there were lots of sergeants and sergeant-majors around to keep
discipline. I was just a corporal. And that's what I'd stay as long as I

was a prisoner. There were no promotions in the prison camps, at least none I ever saw. I heard later—rumour?—that some NCOs had been promoted while prisoners, but I never saw it, and I really didn't care one way or another at the time.

The camp was called Fallingbostal. It's still there. It was about ten miles away from Brunswick, as far as I can tell. Cold. It was located at the end of a dirt road with heavy fortifications all around. Our particular compound was a recent addition to an already enormous prison camp with more prisoners in the next compounds and with space between the compounds. A huge area was involved altogether. There were heavy metal gates at the opening and there were guards everywhere. It seemed to me that we had one guard for every prisoner, but I know it couldn't have been.

Within each compound, long wooden huts surrounded a large dirt square area, something of a quadrangle, and these huts were each partitioned inside so that these areas became small rooms with their own entrances. Each long hut had six smaller of these rooms, and in each room were six double bunks, one on top of the other. Each bed had two straw palliasses, and wooden slats to hold the palliasses. We had to burn the slats in the winter in the stove in the middle of the room in order to get any kind of warmth. The palliasse was really just a bag shaped liked a mattress and stuffed with straw, and the straw turned to dust very quickly. So we got these palliasses and put them on our bunks. No one made a fuss. They also gave each of us a coarse brown blanket. That was our bedding. No pillow, of course. We had nothing. Most of us used our clothes or shoes to make a pillow. I got hold of some wooden clogs, Dutch type, which didn't make a good pillow. We all slept in our clothes, which quickly became threadbare and torn. A table with a bench on each side sat in the center of the room, so we had a place to sit and read if we could ever find any books, or eat if we happened to have any grub. The guards locked us in each night when it got dark, or whenever they felt like it.

The Germans told the senior men among us what to do, and these men then gave the rest of us our orders. This made sense, of course, since the British NCOs knew us and knew how to deal with us. One of our guys, a staff sergeant, nice fellow, instructed us that the Germans ordered eight in each hut. "Sort yourselves out," he said, and he left us to ourselves. I'd already met a few other prisoners who had been held in Italy, so we got a couple others and formed a hut. All the men were doing something similar. It was a bit of a jumble, but it finally got done. Some Australians ended up among us, but they pretty much stayed together. The Germans assigned each hut a number and we went inside and tried to find a way to make the place work for us.

Of course, everyone went for one bunk or another. I was responsible for our hut, and I just said, "Let it go, guys. Don't worry about who sleeps where. Just get along." We then had some time to sit down and talk. We really tried to help each other, to do our best. That worked all right for a time. Of course about all we talked about was food. When? How much? What kind? Just food. We were starving. We didn't know when we'd get to eat.

At least in this camp there was a toilet area, although it was just a long room with space along the side for putting your backside. These weren't toilets as we know them. Our guys decided we'd try to make our space as clean and comfortable as possible. Lots of guys were in bad shape, mostly with bowel problems. It was horrible, but all of us were doing our best. Horrible.

We hadn't been in our hut more than a couple hours when we heard someone outside hollering: "Food! There's food coming! In the compound center!" And zoom! Everyone was through the door and heading out for the center, trying not to knock each other down as we ran. And this time there was food, but it came with a price. What the bastards did was open the gates and bring in big dustbins full of what you'd loosely call food. It was a sloshy kind of stew, mostly just gravy with lots of bits and pieces, and we didn't want to know what the bits and pieces consisted of. The rotten and wicked thing they did to us, though, was put these dustbins in various parts of the compound and then they held us back, wouldn't let us near them. When they finally "released" us, let us go for the food, naturally we raced to it in a mad rush. It could have caused fights. We were like animals. Everyone was starving.

And then those scoundrels brought photographers in to the compound to take photographs of us and to put the pictures in the papers to show the public how the British behaved. We were set up. It was ridiculous. These were the people who wanted to beat us? Aaaggghhhh. I never saw the photographs, but I heard about it later. I ate something, though, got something into my stomach. It could have been a dead rat for all I knew, but I didn't care. Those of us who managed to eat got sick, of course. We gorged ourselves and our stomachs couldn't handle it. It was badly done, a real horror. But to tell the truth, it just made our resolve all the stronger. They'd never beat us, we knew that. Not these animals.

Survival as a Prisoner

When you're a prisoner, you're always looking for things. Anything to help make your life better. You steal, if you have to, but you don't steal from a fellow prisoner. None of the prisoners ever stole from one another, as far as I could tell. No one had much, in the first place. If you got a parcel from home, it was filled with the things your family had sent you. If you were lucky it came intact. Sometimes it had been torn apart and the Germans had taken whatever was of value. The Germans didn't have much, either, you know. Not that I'm excusing them. I'm not. Of course the Swiss came around and asked about how we were treated, but not much came of those visits.

Or you just find things. You're always looking for anything to improve your life. I managed to get hold of a tunic that looked as though it belonged to a musician. It was marvelous. Lots of pockets. And I wore a pair of trousers that were actually jodhpurs, buttons and all. I don't remember now where I got those trousers, but I got a lot of good wear from them.

We complained about our supplies through our warrant officers, and the Germans got hold of a whole load of Dutch clogs. No socks, but clogs. I'd seen pictures of clogs before, but I'd never really seen any. So I got a pair. And when our senior NCOs told the Germans we needed socks, the Germans laughed. Eventually they sent in a load of cloth and we learned to wrap that around our feet. You learned how to fold it so it was as comfortable as it could be. You folded it so it was smooth where it counted, and then you put your clogs on, and that was it. The rest of the cloth flopped around outside the clog. We used to wear them to work, everywhere, like that. It was cold and damp. This was winter in northwestern Germany.

The clogs were terribly uncomfortable, but at least they kept my feet from the ground. After a couple more months, I got a pair of what you'd loosely call shoes. I can't tell you where I got them. Don't remember. Somewhere along the way I managed to get them, though. I didn't wear the clogs any more than I had to. I walked around bare foot instead. Shoes. You never appreciate shoes so much as you do in circumstances like that.

I got a couple packs from home. Some fellows didn't get any. I always asked Mum for socks and that helped a lot. I actually got some. You had to feel sorry for the blokes who didn't get packages. They really suffered. Those socks felt good, made a big difference.

There were over a thousand prisoners in our compound, the English-speaking compound—British, Australian, New Zealanders, some South Africans, but no Americans, though I don't know why. Scots. Irish, Welsh. That was our compound. The camp itself was very large, maybe a mile across. I was there nearly two years and never saw all of it. There were other compounds nearby which were separated from us by barbed wire, and I never got into any of them. It was a high wire, twenty feet or more. About six feet away from this wire was a trip wire, and that was as far as we were allowed to go. If you put your foot over that wire, you were open game. They would figure you were trying to escape. We all felt the Germans were just looking for a reason to shoot. It would release their frustration. If you gave them an excuse, you could get killed. I'm not saying every German was a killer just waiting to shoot; there were good Germans and bad Germans, same as everybody else. But, well, you just didn't set your foot across that line.

I saw one guy get shot, but he wasn't killed. He'd been fooling around playing catch and he was going after a tennis ball. He just crossed over chasing the ball, as if he wasn't even thinking about it. He probably wasn't.

We were lucky, though, from what I understand. Other Allied troops were in much worse shape than we were, had it a lot harder. The Americans especially. I saw some Americans at times, and they were always in a bad way. Really bad. And other Allied prisoners in camps farther east were apparently much worse off than we were. We heard rumours, of course. And I read about it after the war.

Our camp was in the middle of Germany, not far from Berlin. There are no two prison camps alike, from what I can tell. When I spoke after the war with other prisoners-of-war, I discovered they were better or worse off than we were. It seemed to have a lot to do with the officers in charge of the camp. I thought we were badly treated in the camp in Germany, and we were. But at least we were able to wash and keep ourselves reasonably clean. That mattered. Plus we slept on bunks, for what that's worth. I know of other Allied prisoners of war who were farther east in German prisoner-of-war camps, and I consider myself fortunate. Although the camp I was in wasn't pleasant, by any stretch of the imagination, I heard stories of prisoners in other camps who were made to work in salt mines, in the muck, never dry, in shocking conditions.

The Daily Life

On our second day at the prison camp we were sent to work and we passed a group of women walking along slowly, heading in the same direction, also going to work. They were obviously in pain. They were a mixture of ages, but they were all wearing striped outfits which looked like pajamas, and they all had their heads shaved. This was in the winter. We stood there, confused. Why were they like this? We knew they were prisoners, of course, but we didn't know what we were seeing, didn't realize at the time about Germany's horrible persecution of the Jews. The women stopped. They were all carrying something, like a sack filled with something, and one of them couldn't lift it any longer. The guards hit the woman until she picked up her pack. Women guards. We wanted to help, naturally, but our guards stopped us. We couldn't believe what we were seeing. I knew right then that this camp would be different from what I'd experienced before in Italy and even in North Africa.

I've read since the war about informants in prison camps, but I'm certain they never got into our huts. We would have spotted them quickly. We were aware of any person who seemed odd. The Germans got very little information from the prisoners, from what I could tell. We had a guard who used to walk into the hut friendly like and tried to befriend us and talk silly things, tried to finagle information out of us. We told him so much garbage that he gave up. We'd tell him whatever we could make up that sounded intriguing. At first he fell for it, and we'd all have a good laugh later. We'd whisper nonsense into his shell-like ears. Not too bright, those sentries.

I heard that most Allied prisoners either were held in the prison camps or were sent out to do farm work or industrial work. The Germans didn't seem to care what work they gave us as long as they could get some sort of labor from us. Their country was definitely shorthanded at the time, so they figured we were a type of slave for them. They often gave us jobs against all the rules of the Geneva Convention. We were not supposed to work in factories or in any kind of bombing target, but the Germans didn't care. We were less than nothing to them.

My comrades and myself were forced to do anything heavy and dirty. We were required to get inside the ovens and rake out all the cinders and dirt that remained after the steel was made. It was hot and miserable from the fumes, and we could hardly breathe while we worked. It also burnt the hell out of our footwear. Once we told the guards we weren't going to do it. We planned to go on strike. We used bad language toward them. The vorarbeiter shouted a lot but he was a little wary. I guess we were past their threats, though, because we held our ground. To our surprise, it worked, at least for a while, and we were given a different kind of work building huts for Russian prisoners nearby. We always messed with whatever they had us do, of course, trying to weaken whatever they had us construct. The cement we mixed, for example, wasn't going to last very long.

The huts were mostly prefabricated and we assembled them, too. We were given no food all day, just water and sometimes a coup of ersatz coffee, bloody awful. We just sat down at lunch times and saw the civilians eating. Some prisoners, especially the French and Belgians, were allowed to go to work by themselves, no guards watching; so they had more chances to obtain bread or vegetables or whatever they might need. Their countries were occupied, of course, so they didn't dare try escaping. Their families were threatened. We were given soup in the evening and we shared some black bread, but that was about it. If any of us had received a food parcel, it would usually be split up all around and we'd make a kind of stew with lots of water in it to fill and satisfy us to a degree. We all thought of food day and night, every man there.

We had to walk about six kilometers to work, so it took us an hour or so. We all went to the Hermann Goehring Steelworks, even the European prisoners. Hundreds of people worked there. They lied to us and told us we were making toys, since it was against the Geneva Convention for us to be making munitions, but we knew we weren't making toys. We saw huge ingots put on trains and taken out of the factory. The vorarbeiter distributed the work each day.

I was a prisoner-of-war, and that was that. A simple soldier, no rank. We did have among us a sergeant-major who had it all, the clothes and the words and everything. You had to respond when this bloke opened his mouth. He was a lot like my former sergeant-major, Thomas Bubble, Old Tommy, the man who moved me from civilian life to military life. Old Tommy was the kind of man you read about in the comics, and he was definitely my idea of a proper sergeant-major. If he'd been a prisoner-of-war, he'd have let the camp know his rank, who he was. He had that charisma. He was the smartest man I ever saw, as tough as old boots.

We also had a quartermaster sergeant—three stripes and a crown, a staff sergeant, but with technical rank so he was a quartermaster, in charge of the stores—this guy was first rate. He let everybody know his rank, but he did it in a quiet manner. When we first arrived in the camp, the Germans came in and wanted to know who were the NCOs. I didn't say a word. You can have it, I thought. But this man—seemed like an office man—he looked at them and said, rather quietly, "I'm a quartermaster sergeant." So he was a sergeant-major. They don't mess around with any quartermaster. So there he was, senior NCO in the compound.

What used to annoy me with him was when we'd have a meeting and a German officer would come in to speak. This bloody fellow used to try to connect his name with the German names. His name sounded somewhat German. He'd say, "I'm trying to work this out. I have something of a German name." He thought he'd do well with the Germans because he had a German name. He seemed to be trying to impress them with his bloody name. He was too daft to see they didn't care a fig for his name. I asked him about it, tried to suggest that he was off on the wrong tack with them, but he didn't seem to pay any attention.

Then this fellow who reminded me of Sergeant-Major Tommie came in. He was a paratrooper, actually was a sergeant-major. Quite a brave bloke, a real tough man. He'd tried to fight the Germans by himself, we learned, got involved in some major fire-fights. He was one of those you could spot real easy. No question. He was a hard John Wayne type, that sort. He could do anything, and you knew it as soon as he came into the camp. We'd never seen those paratroopers with their classy red berets until they came in as prisoners. I'm telling you, though, that this chap didn't act like a prisoner. "I know what I want and I know what I like!" he'd yell out. And the Germans were bloody frightened of him. Because he had that way. He came into camp and took over. "Well, I'm here now and I'm in charge." That sort of thing. And nobody said, "No, you're not." The quartermaster-sergeant with the German name pretty much faded away. And the sergeant-major just took over the camp, and he was good. We got more with him being in charge than ever before. "Well, I want to speak to your guard commander, whatever his name is," he'd tell the Germans. And they'd take him to the CO, just as he'd demanded.

He was of the sort who believed in strict discipline, very strict. It was balmy, but he commanded bloody respect. I saw German guards shy away if he was around. And he knew it: "We're not going to have these silly bastards near us." And he had that piercing voice. Everybody knew he was there. He couldn't actually do a damned thing, no more than I could do or you could do. We didn't have any real authority about us. But he had it about him.

And that's why we won the bloody war: We had people like him. I think of Harry Truman when I think of him. He wasn't a big man, but he had something about him such that you knew he was in charge. "The buck stops here!" This fellow was like that. He never could care less about them. He wouldn't think twice about standing up to them.

We were restricted to our huts at night, of course. We couldn't be out after eight o'clock. They actually locked us in. If you had to go to the toilet, which was outside the huts, you made sure you went before eight. In the morning the guards would open up and yell and shout at us to get up and get out. And we'd run out of the hut clutching our clothes.

Mail
We were allowed to have mail but we wrote our letters in a kind of language that only our parents or other loved ones would understand.

The Germans subjected every letter sent or received to the blue pencil. It happened both ways, of course. The British looked over my parents' letters; the Germans looked over ours. Once I told my parents about the air raids on our camps—both the Brits and the Americans flew over regularly—and it never got crossed out because of the code. For example, we'd use the word *Brylcreem*, that gel for your hair, to refer to the RAF because they were the envy of us all. They had the best of everything and always looked sharp. So we just called them Brylcreem Boys. Mom and Dad would know what I meant if I wrote that I'd seen some of the boys with Brylcreem. Mom and Dad would know an air raid had gone on. I don't remember how these code words got started, or how the code got passed around, but we all did it, one way or another.

In theory, we could get mail from anyone who sent it. Usually it was on a printed piece of stationery with a flap in it, but the writer couldn't seal it or the government wouldn't send it. The Germans actually gave us paper and pen so we could write. But what could you tell your parents? You could tell them you're okay, and that's about it. If not, the German censors would cross it out. You couldn't let your parents or anyone know you were having a bad time. You might say, in code, that you need something: Needle and thread? They'd send clothes. They'd send food parcels sometimes. Might be some left, too, after the Germans got to it. Prisoners would also occasionally get food parcels from British services.

Cigarettes were money. You'd use them the exact same way you used money. Germans would buy them or trade for them because the cigarettes in Germany were so horrible. Trading cigarettes became one of the only ways to actually pick anything up that wasn't issued, so we always appreciated receiving cigarettes in a package from home. They'd also get pilfered, of course, by the guards checking the packages. Food parcels, naturally, were appreciated all the time, all the time. You lived on rumours of food coming. Rumours gave you hope even though nothing ever happened. They gave a promise for tomorrow. "I hear the Allies are making advances," or, "There's some food coming." If you heard a truck, you were sure it would contain food parcels. Like a mirage in a desert. You had the hope that the rumour might be right this one time, but it wasn't. Ever. Still it kept you going, kept you sane, in a weird way.

Learning the Tricks

It's amazing what you can discover among people who have been wandering around dirty and smelly and worrying about what they're going to eat, people you wouldn't expect to know how to do anything but scrounge, especially anything artistic. Do we have a musician among us? Do we need a piano? A trumpet? You ask around about music and you find that the last person in the world you'd think could play a trumpet is a blooming virtuoso. You had to get instruments, of course, but it's really not as hard as you'd think. At first it's, "There's no way in hell that I can get a trumpet." And if you continue thinking that way you'll never get it. "What can we do to get one?" That's the attitude. So you sit around and talk about the situation, and people come out with all kinds of suggestions, some crazy and some pretty logical. Of course there's a lot of it swearing in such discussions, but the swearing itself is a kind of relief under these circumstances.

So you say, where are we? What's our situation, exactly? You're in a room with a few others and you have nothing. No books. Nothing. But if you sit down and say, "Look, we're a bunch of idiots or we wouldn't be here, so let's work something out even if we make a mess, let's do something we can remember." Soon you start offering something different for people who are just annoyed at life, something to divert their attention. And things start changing. "Let's get a blooming trumpet and see if we can make music," you say. That's the way to do it.

Music is wonderful. Music makes up for a lack of food, drink, clean clothes, showers, everything. It has an amazing effect. Finally we found three or four fellows who could really play. One was a Scotsman who could pick up anything and make it sound beautiful, one of those guys. This bloke claimed he could play a trumpet, but of course nobody had ever heard him. We challenged him, gave him a bad time, said we doubted that he could play; and he just said, "So find me a bloody horn." Well, we got one. Got drums, too, and later found a flute player and a clarinet player. We even found a piano player, but of course where would we ever get a piano? But damned if we didn't find one. A piano! Can you imagine?

We started with the small things. A cornet is smaller than a trumpet, and a cornet will do. So we approached the guard for our room. We asked ourselves, are we willing to sacrifice some cigarettes, some soap, maybe even a pair of socks for a musical instrument?

We talked to him and said we wanted to put together a musical group, and we asked him if he could help. We even told him we'd invite him in to listen. After a couple weeks, he came back—he'd been out and had met others, had had time to think about our offer—cigarettes meant a lot, remember—and he'd found someone with an old cornet. So we collected all around and made it happen. We got it. It happened with a snare drum, too, and a side drum, a flute, even a clarinet.

But how could we get a piano? The NCO did some talking to the guard—"We'll do what you want," he said, "no argument; we'll cooperate. We won't give you a hard time," etc.—and it worked. I think the key was that the commanding officer thought we'd keep off his back if we had some sort of diversion.

We came back to the hut one day after working all day and there was a piano sitting in the center of the room. We really couldn't believe it. We all laughed hard about it. Amazing. A piano, right there. So now we had a band. A *band*. The guys would finish working, would gobble down some food, and then they'd start playing music. They played well, too. We had music and it was great. Of course we couldn't change our clothes, couldn't eat very well, certainly couldn't get our freedom. But we had music.

We arranged for a concert, but we had to ask permission since we weren't supposed to congregate. In the meantime, a few of us tried to work out a way to take some of the piss out of the Germans. We decided to dress up as near as we could to look just like them, like the German guards and officers. Then we could make fun of them without doing anything but a bit of mugging. So we circled the camp looking for tailors, designers, anyone who could handle clothing. And we found them. They made German uniforms out of blankets, old gray-green blankets. It turned out to be a real piss-taker, but the Germans didn't really recognize what was happening. We made fun of them and they didn't even recognize it. We had a great time, though.

The Germans, as far as I can tell, could never make head nor tail of the British. My sense was that they all thought we were a bit balmy. But being balmy is a good way out of being depressed. For the concert, for example, we had one guy who could sing and another guy who was as funny as anyone I've ever seen—named Jimmy Lee—he was very good. He made it big later in show business. He was the organizer of our program, and he was great. We had a few Australians among us, not many, and some New Zealand soldiers, all tough fellows, but mostly we were all English.

Our camp even came up with a couple records, and a record player. It was an old wind-up job and it went from hut to hut. Of course the needles we used didn't last long. I tried to use pins we'd gathered over time, but that didn't do much good. We only had two records: "The Sunny Side of the Street" and "Let Bygones Be Bygones and Start All Over Again," both by Izzy Bonn, from London. It was all very nostalgic stuff those days, and of course that music always got us thinking about home. Eventually the record player wore out, but I shall never forget it. It really added some life to that death-dream.

We didn't have many such diversions, I'm afraid. We just didn't have the energy to see such projects through. Also we weren't able to do much sensible thinking. We were just too hungry and tired all the time. You had to be at least somewhat fit for such enterprises, and so much of our time—when we weren't working outside—was spent trying to sleep hunger thoughts away. We were in bad shape without food all day, so we didn't have much spunk. It was because of this that we weren't able to get much participation in sports like cricket, football, baseball, basketball. I've heard of prison camps where they had organized such sports, but it didn't happen at Fallingbostal.

Of course, we played card games as often as possible, even to the point of creating homemade cards, and we did other things to amuse ourselves and to pass the time. All the prisoners loved to play checkers and chess, for example, and some fellows did put together a kind of cricket match one time after negotiating a couple of tennis balls while they were at work (trading English cigarettes) and after carving a cricket bat out of a hunk of firewood. We were always watched by guards, though, even during the games, and we'd be put on restrictions if we ever got out of sight.

In spite of the card-playing and all the other sports events, I can't remember any real gambling among the prisoners in Germany. We were without gambling money, of course, or anything else of value, so any gambling would have to be with chits which might be redeemable back in England some day, or maybe with cigarettes. But I never saw gambling. We were issued some funny camp money, but there was nothing to buy in the camp in Germany except salt and ersatz soap.

Prisoners told and re-told jokes, corny and stale jokes, until they were no good anymore. Frankly, jokes were not in such great demand; stories were. Anyone who could tell a good story became a camp hero. We longed for stories about nearly anything, the true and the made-up, the preposterous and the mundane. So much of it was in the telling.

Men would talk of escape, of course, but not too loudly. Prisoners mostly talked of their work that day, what they'd done. We loved to hear about taking the piss out of the enemy, always that. We all had great satisfaction whenever we heard a story like that. And some of the guys would talk about God or what their mothers used to make for dinner, or breakfast, or dessert. We all loved to talk about food. It took us back to those times when we had more than enough to fill our stomachs. Naturally we began to recognize how much we had taken for granted, not just the food but the warmth, the cleanliness, the closeness of family and friends. Now we were in a place where we'd sometimes get so hungry that we'd chew pieces of wood like chewing gum.

The Germans were never far away, of course. They guarded us more closely in camp than anywhere else. I guess that must be a compliment, so we played games with the "square-heads," our term for the guards. They never seemed to recognize comedy. Or maybe they just didn't want to laugh with us, afraid it would put them on our level. We all really enjoyed taking the piss out of the German guards whenever we could, though. If they'd walk into our hut, we'd act as though we were up to something, scurrying about and pretending to hide things. We'd make a face to get them riled up. But of course it was nothing. We just enjoyed the little laugh we'd get from it.

We always had books, strangely enough. Sometimes your family would send books, but not often. Mostly you wanted food from your family. People would pass books back and forth, sometimes from hut to hut. Most prisoners were generous in giving other prisoners things they needed when possible. Reading material, writing material, whatever. And of course these prisoners would do the same. You'd return things you'd borrow. People were good about that.

The prisoners, of course, came from a variety of lifestyles and professions, and we sometimes would occasionally organize get-togethers in one or another of the huts by setting up committees for special reasons. One of the committees might be for entertainment, and the members would wander from hut to hut asking for people to talk about their pre-war jobs and what kind of life they had: Were you a postman, a policeman, a teacher, a lawyer, etc.? One guy was an ex-convict, and he entertained us all with stories about his life in prison (not that different from where we were in Germany, of course). He constantly talked about escape, hated the camp. But he told great stories. We also enjoyed the policeman's stories of being on the beat and how he'd encountered various infamous villains and gangsters.

One of the prisoners was a fairly well-known boxer who used to enthrall us with recounts of some of his fights. One time he even challenged the commanding officer of the German guardsmen to a little friendly match between the guards and a few of us. I liked the idea, but it didn't occur. Probably a good thing since we were in such bad shape that we might well have been killed. Hard to say, though. We had a lot of spirit, a strong desire to strike out at the guards. But how long we would have lasted was anyone's guess.

A couple Australians from one of the huts told us tales of the outback life, filled with encounters with alligators and Aborigines. Probably most of the tales had been made up, but we didn't care. We also had some South Africans, with their unusual accents, who loved talking about their good life in Cape Town and around. They also liked to sing little African ditties. They were nice fellows, and we always got along well with them. Sometimes they spoke Afrikaans to each other, though, which put some of us off. They just wanted their own private conversations, I guess.

We all talked about history quite a bit, kicked around whatever we knew, or thought we knew. And some of the guys tried to study languages, German mostly. A few could speak French, too, and were willing to teach others. Italian also seemed to be a popular language to learn, and some of us had picked up a bit of that earlier so we tried to pass on what we knew.

As you'd expect, some guys loved to talk of their conquests with the women. I'm sure some of that was wishful thinking, but the stories were still worth listening to. At that time, though, we were all too hungry to really crave sex. I think a sweet little filly might have been eaten instead.

When anyone received a letter from home—this was rare but it happened occasionally—and if the receiver wanted to talk about it or share it, this person got everyone's attention. Others listened very quietly and reverently, even though the letters were read by the censors before the owner got hold of them, and anything the Germans didn't want you to read had been blacked out. But we knew. Those days, when some fellows were fortunate enough to get a letter, those were good days. It was nice to be thought of kindly by your loved ones, and nice to share.

If you got a food parcel, life felt pretty good. These were designed for one prisoner, and you wouldn't expect to get one a week, of course. But when you got one, it was supposed to last one man for a week. If you were clever and strict with yourself, you knew how to stretch it out. I only ever had a complete food parcel all to myself a couple times, both in Italy. In Germany you really had to share them just out of consideration. You'd divide it maybe one for eight. If you had a tin of meat, you shared it. When do you open it? Which day? What time of the day? These were key questions.

As far as I know, we only received one Red Cross parcel in the entire German compound during the time I was in this camp, and it had to be shared among fifteen men. These parcels had been sent to Switzerland by the American and British Red Cross to help keep the prisoners well. At one parcel to each man, that gives you an idea of the size of the parcels. Of course one per man would have been very generous, but most never reached prisoner-of-war camps.

All the time I was imprisoned, from January of 1944 to April of 1945, the Germans were in trouble themselves. I never saw a well-fed guard. If any parcels from England got to the prisoners, the guards would be willing to swap for things. Usually our parcels were pilfered, ransacked by the guards before we got hold of them. Often they didn't arrive at our huts at all.

I saw some prisoners who were foolish enough to want cigarettes more than food. I was a smoker myself, but I'm thankful that the smoking wasn't as important as food. Some seemed to be able to cope better with a smoke than with food, however. What can I say? If you ate a bread roll, it was gone in five minutes. If you smoked a cigarette, maybe it would last ten minutes. These sorts of things seemed to make a difference. Those men sometimes became ill and didn't make it.

Stealing Food

The routine the Germans developed for us to get food—after that first scandalous day—was to choose two men to pick up the supplies twice each day. These men were to stand outside the huts each morning and each evening, holding a blanket. Two men per hut. They were assembled in strict military fashion, and they'd be counted about ten times. Then they'd march through the gate with German guards beside them, right through the gate and to the cookhouse. This cookhouse catered to the prisoners and the staff, anyone in that compound.

Each man then took a turn picking up food. We all wanted to get this duty because we always thought maybe we'd get a chance to pinch something. People who worked in the cookhouse would throw food into the blanket, whatever they had that they thought we should have. Then, when you'd got what you were entitled to, the guards checked it all over. You went outside and stood there until all the other men came out. It took awhile, and it meant about ten men from five huts would be inside the cookhouse together.

I usually went in with a Scotsman, Tom Ramsey, a special guy, a former military policeman, a brute. He had a big growth on his cheek, very red and poisonous. But he ignored it. He was a lance corporal in the military police. Big guy. We used to walk around the compound together when we weren't working, and we'd talk a lot. He was a hard but kind man. He and I started talking about the possibility of pinching some food, and we finally decided to quit talking about it and to go ahead and do it.

This is a story I'm very proud of because it was a way of sticking it to the Germans. Here's how it happened: Tom and I decided to get into the cookhouse and get extra food. Maybe we'd get shot, but we really didn't give a damn. The idea was to get in there and beat the Germans. We wanted to beat them any way we could. We took a few months to plan our raid and we never told anyone else for a long time. We walked and talked about it. And we laughed. Just planning it gave us a good feeling, even if we'd never accomplished it.

The plan was that we'd cause some commotion in the ranks while all the guys formed up to get the food. That's how we'd get it going. We finally told a couple others about it since we realized we'd need their help.

We intended to bring along two blankets, instead of one. The two blankets were no problem. We also had to get two extra men from our hut going out for the food. Then we had to confuse the Germans as we were going through the gate so they wouldn't be able to take an accurate count. Tom and I talked about it many times, in detail. We knew which German guards were daft and probably couldn't count, so we waited until it was their turn to oversee the food collection. We fooled about among the ranks before we went for it. We figured we just had to keep folks moving. We'd shift the men from the front to the back, and back again. Finally the guards would say, "Hey! Let it go." Then they'd just leave us. "Go on," they'd say. They'd throw their arms up and let us go. They couldn't win. But it was just another routine to them, just a boring duty, and they wanted to get it over with. That's what we were counting on.

I know this doesn't sound possible, but this is what happened. We got most of the fellows from our hut to come outside, skylark about, make a lot of noises like it was all fun in games. The guards didn't know what was going on. They ordered us in and we all came out again. Finally Tom and I went out, carrying blankets, with the blokes collecting the food. We had at least half a dozen guys creating havoc, just trying to distract the guards. The order of the day was confusion. Create chaos. Distraction. And we got away with it. Tom and I just looked at each other as we went on into the cookroom, and we tried to keep from laughing.

What we had to do after that was hide somewhere inside the cookroom. That was the next big challenge. We'd been in and out several times in the past, of course, and we had our ideas of where we'd hide. I got in a cupboard, and Tom slipped under a table. We pretty much knew ahead of time just where we'd hide, though. Tom had the blankets. I didn't know if we'd get away with it, but I kept thinking, What's the worst thing that they could do? I knew they wouldn't kill us. They might beat us up and send us to the brig, but that's about the worst. But what we didn't know was when the cooks went home. We didn't have any idea about this, but we were aware that the cookhouse ordinarily closed after we left.

So we were in this room—it was a big room where you could really vanish. And finally we heard the others all marching off. We were in there, all right, but the cooks were there too. They were cleaning up. We had to be quiet for a long time. It seemed like hours. They were talking, laughing, mostly just finishing up for the day and setting things up for the next day. Finally, probably thirty minutes to an hour later, they left and locked up. No one remained. It was dark, of course, and we couldn't see a damned thing, and of course we couldn't turn on any lights. But we knew where stuff was because we'd been there enough times and we'd paid attention.

We took as much as we could. We didn't do it secretly, so they wouldn't know. We wanted them to know. We really wanted them to see that they'd been had. We ate all those things we couldn't ordinarily get. Anything slightly fresh, like fruit and vegetables. I got sick, in fact. And we filled the blanket as full as we could and still carry it. Then we tied it in a knot and hid it where we could pick it up the next morning. We then took turns pissing on all the food we knew was assigned for the Germans only.

The next morning the cooks showed up and, of course, we got out of sight. By then, we'd found better hiding places near the door so we could blend right in when the prisoners arrived. We worried that the cooks might notice that things had been altered, but they didn't show any recognition of it. Must have been because they just never ever thought about such an act. A short time later, the prisoners came in and got coffee and black bread, and we just came out of hiding and slipped in with the group of them. Ersatz bread and ersatz coffee. The bread filled our blanket. It took up space. The other blokes from our hut came with their blankets, and we all left the cookhouse as though we'd just walked in. We didn't let them put any bread in their blankets, though. We already had the bread. We threw it in and put our blanket along with theirs. Our hut's blanket was twice as big as anyone else's, and I couldn't see how we'd get away with it. The guys just threw their bread into our blankets. The bloody thing was heavy. But we confused the guards again and managed to get out. I still can't believe we made it. War does that, though. It makes you go for things you might otherwise pass up. I think now that part of the reason we got away with it is that nobody could believe anyone would try something like that. It was too blatant an act, too ridiculous.

We went back to the hut and opened the blanket up and all our guys laughed their heads off. I told them if anyone talked about this, we'd all suffer. Our attitude to the Germans was, "Tough luck." They did find out, of course, just as we'd hoped they would. But we didn't want to get caught, of course, and we sure as hell didn't want to lose the food. So we pulled up the floorboard and hid the food in holes we'd prepared ahead of time, putting dirt and soil back on top.

Pretty soon, we heard screams and shouts outside. The Germans went a little nuts from their anger. I remember the guards and officers went straight into a meeting. Then they started banging on doors to the huts. Fortunately, none of the prisoners from the other huts knew what was happening.

The guards ordered us all to the grounds and the senior officer started screaming about what they'd do to us, and so on. I got nervous, of course, but I didn't let on. Eventually men came in and searched every hut in order to find where the food was. They didn't find it, but they knew it was around. The rest of the prisoners eventually learned what had happened—even though they didn't all know which hut had done it—and of course all loved it. The Germans never did find out it was our hut. We ate like bloody animals for a few days.

The Germans never ever let up, though. They knew it was us prisoners, but they couldn't prove which ones. Mostly they were so angry that they had been beaten this way, and they were frustrated because there was nothing they could do, really. They couldn't restrict us from privileges since they hadn't given us any privileges to be taken away. I believe if they'd found it was Tom and I, they'd have given us additional labor, prodded us with their rifles, and put us in cells for a few nights with no food or bedding. But they never did discover who pulled it off.

We did it for the joy of the attempt as much as anything else. We really didn't care if we were caught. We just wanted to beat them. And we did.

A Fight

I hit someone once, a civilian working for the Germans. I couldn't have done it if he'd been a guard. I'd have been shot in about five minutes. It happened one morning while I was in a small group of prisoners who been marched to a place where the Germans wanted to build a new compound for more prisoners, for some Russian prisoners. We were mixing cement for the carpenters, also prisoners, to use in the building of the new huts. I was wearing a pair of old boots, very old boots, not much life in them. Remember that a person's shoes are very important in a prison camp.

I was in the latrine cleaning the cement off them because I knew the cement would eat them away and I wanted to keep them decent. I had asked my foreman, a Hungarian, a kind man, if I could go and wash off my boots. He said, "Sure, but no funny business." I said, "No, of course." Never take liberties, I felt, if they gave you a break. So I went into the latrine to wash the cement off my shoes. I stood there and put my foot up on the side of a trough, the sort of trough you'd use to feed a pig. The water came into it from pipes, dirty water good for cleaning or flushing, but that was about all.

So I put my foot on the trough and let the water run over my boot. Suddenly I heard this voice in the doorway, and I looked up and saw this man in a uniform, a German civilian worker there at the site. I pretended I didn't understand him, but actually I did. He asked me for my identity papers. I just carried on, as if he hadn't spoken, and I went back to what I was doing. I thought, *No, I won't acknowledge you, you bastard. You talk to my guard and I'll have to listen, but I don't have to listen to you.* I just wasn't in the mood for it, frankly. But I heard his steps approach me, so I turned around and there he was. He reminded me of a man who worked at a railroad station back home, sort of official looking, standing there in his uniform—but everyone was in uniform at that time. He was wearing a pistol, so I guessed he was some special kind of guard. He started shouting, like the Germans sometimes do, demanding my identity papers.

And all I said was, *"Nichts verstehen"* ("I don't understand"). He didn't stop, so I shouted, *"Nichts verstehen!!"* I went back to finishing what I was doing, went on washing, realizing that my guard knew what I was doing and I didn't have to have anyone else's permission. I knew I was okay. This guy didn't say anything else to me, just stood there, so I thought I'd got rid of him. But I hadn't. As I washed, suddenly, *Pow!* I got this punch, full force, right on my ear. He sent me clean across the room and I went down in a lump. He'd knocked me silly when I wasn't expecting it. My ear was bleeding and I was just lying in the corner of the latrine, humiliated and in pain. I was angry, just saw red. I don't know how I got up or how I recovered. All I know is I found myself on my feet and I knew I had to get back at him. These guys were used to being bullies and I'm sure he expected me to just lie there and take it.

I should have done the sensible thing and gone to my *vorarbeiter* (my foreman) and said, "That man hit me." Just that. I should have told him right away. Not that he would have dealt with it, but at least I'd have done the reasonable thing. But I didn't have the brains. If someone had come around and taken care of the situation, that would have done it. But that wouldn't have been enough for me. I had to do more. Simple as that. I had this thing in my head, and I wasn't alone in this, this sense that no one should treat me like that. But I couldn't get away with any retaliation. That much I knew. I felt I was better than the Germans who were guarding us, though, and certainly better than this man who hit me, whoever he was. That's how it was with me then. I couldn't take much more. It wasn't heroics on my part, just anger, stupidity.

So I shot across the latrine as soon as I recovered and I attacked him. I nearly killed him. My anger was so great that I would have killed him if I'd not been stopped. And I could have, I'm sure. I really wasn't that strong. We weren't being fed well. But I hit him, right in the face. Bang! Smashed his nose. He was bleeding. But I wasn't satisfied. I hit him again and again, couldn't stop. He was in a bad way. He shouted for help, screamed. The others, the several guards, came in and pulled me away from the guy I was beating on. I immediately broke away from the guards and ran off. I can't explain the guards, what they were thinking. All I could think of was getting away. So I took off running. They never shot at me, never even came directly after me. I got to one of the nearby buildings and found a trash can near a low roof, and I climbed right up onto the roof. And I stood there trying to get hold of myself. I was scared and filled with adrenaline.

The incident had raised a major commotion, of course. Others came running out of the building—cooks and kitchen help, we were in that part of the compound—and the guards let the dogs go, German shepherds and Alsatian-type dogs, big, mean creatures. And they were all going after me, barking and jumping at me. My *vorarbeiter* had nothing to do with this, but the guards were shouting at me, threatening me, pointing their guns at me. But one of the guards, thank god, listened to me. I was shouting, "He hit me! That sonuvabitch hit me!" And I showed him the blood on my ear. "He hit me!" And he called at me: "Stay! Stay!" The dogs kept growling and barking, but of course they couldn't reach me.

I decided not to stay there, in spite of what he said. I just didn't quite trust him, and I was still quite frightened. The buildings were close together, so I leaped from roof to roof, just tried to get away. This wasn't logical or sensible since I really had nowhere to go. I was just very angry and very scared, jumping from one roof to another like a madman. I had no idea what was going to happen. I was desperate for a way out. Where could I go? How could I escape? I couldn't. Soon I ran out of roofs. The dogs were right there, of course, since they'd followed me; and the cooks were screaming and waving their pans at me, whatever they had. It was like a bad dream.

Finally that one sane guard waved his rifle and called to me: "Come on down. I'll protect you." He made it clear to me that I was his responsibility. I said, *"Genug?"* ("Enough?") And he said, *"Ya, ya. Genug."*

As I stood there considering my next step, I saw several Germans come out to the hut wearing armband swastikas, so I figured it was all over. I think if it hadn't been for that one guard I'd have been shot right then. He was my protector. So I finally came down, slowly, and stood beside that guard. I felt confident that he'd do what was right. I trusted him. What choice did I have? He was one of those I had spoken to as we were marched to work. He'd told me about his wife and children. We'd made a human contact and I'm sure that's why he was willing to help me this time.

He grabbed my arm and led me into a small administration building where the man in charge was pure SS. He looked just like Erich Von Stroheim. He was sitting on his desk in his perfect uniform with that bloody swastika on his arm. He was Hitler and Himmler and all of them wrapped into one. I was standing there in front of him with two guards, one on each side of me, two ordinary soldiers with green-gray uniforms. They were nothing to him, and I knew I was in serious trouble. This man, an officer, but not the CO of the compound, screamed at me, as they seemed always to do. It seemed to be the main way they communicated. It was frightening. I didn't really understand German well, but I knew he was saying, "You dare hit a German?" He called me all the names he could, "Swine," being the one I remember most. And I had to stand there and take it. I hated it. In the end he said how this was his country and how could I and who did I think I was and this and that. I couldn't understand every word, but I knew I was in a bad situation.

My guard was one-hundred percent on my side. He probably saved my life. We hadn't had much support like that in our time there, and I was surprised to receive it. If I could have, I'd have given him a medal. He did his duty as a soldier, and he took a hell of a risk talking to this maniac officer. He more or less told him, "This is my prisoner," and he held his ground. The officer ranted and raved, but this guard just stood there and never lost his cool, just said, "This is my prisoner." ("*Bit mei.*") I knew enough to realize what he was saying. He said, "You do not touch him." That took courage, in my opinion. That would have been a risky move even within the British military.

The officer had been speaking so hysterically that I really couldn't understand him well. But from his gestures and the sound of his voice, I could tell that he was extremely angry, that he was calling me names, and that he was convinced there was no way I would get away with hitting a German. The guard saw all this going on, and of course he saw it better than I did because he could understand the language, and he did exactly what he said he'd do: He'd said, "I'll protect you." His attitude was that I was his prisoner and he would deal with me through his own officers, and that was that. I thought he'd be afraid to stand up to this officer, but he did. He really did. I looked at this fellow and I thought, That's really good. That's my kind of man. I like that. I'd like to think I would have done that if our situations had been reversed. I hope so.

I am still amazed that he got away with it. I didn't know German military rules, of course. I didn't know how far the officer could go under these circumstances. All I knew was this guard was a bloody brave guy. The officer was obviously very senior and someone to watch out for, but the guard simply said, "This is my prisoner and you don't touch him." And he didn't. He still ranted on, but at the end of it, he just turned to me and said, "Out. March. Out." I walked away thinking he might shoot me at any minute, but nothing happened. I walked out toward the rest of the prisoners, and the *vorarbeiter*, who was there by then, met us outside the office. My fellow prisoners thought it was great, of course, to see that man get hit.

The *vorarbeiter* marched us all back to the hut. That guard came along beside me while I was walking and said to me, and he wasn't smiling or being cute, he just said, in German, but clear enough to me: "You're in trouble." I said, "Yeah." He said, "You're in trouble. I'll speak to the CO, because he'll find out anyway. You just keep quiet." I didn't ask anything.

So we went back to the huts and we were dismissed, and it wasn't long after that two guards came and marched me to the CO's office. And when I got there, the guard who had been with me all the time was talking with the CO. I don't know what the CO's rank was, something like a colonel, and he sat there and looked me up and down, no expression. He spoke a little English, and he looked at me and said, "You know what you've done. You know the rules. You just don't touch. That's all there is to it. This is our army." I knew in England we'd punish such an act by putting the man in a cell for a while. So I expected I'd get something like that. All they could do was give me more time in a prison camp. What would that hurt? The CO wasn't nasty, but he was serious. He just said, "You were out of line. You can't just come into Germany and hit a German citizen." He went on and on. He said the guard told him there was some provocation, but he added that as an English soldier I should be above that. "But obviously you're not, so you'll go into the cell."

I just stood there and felt like saying, "Thank you very much." That wasn't bad. I had thought it could be much worse, but I didn't know what it would be.

So that night I stayed in the cell. For one night. That was it. And the truth is I was fed better that night than I'd ever been fed outside the cell. I didn't know how long I'd be there, but I only stayed one bloody night. The food was very good because there was a Frenchman and two Belgians in there with me and they had food parcels which they shared with me. I don't know what they'd done, but this wasn't bad, I tell you.

I never heard anything more about this, except some of the other prisoners rode me about it a bit. Old Tough Mayhead, you know, that sort of rot. And somebody usually wants to take you apart when you stand out like that. They just can't stand it. You always find somebody who wants to make sure he's tougher than you are.

I never saw the German I hit again. I don't know what happened to him. You have to realize that your mind gets poisoned while you're there. You just let it build up. You don't feel that what's happened is fair, and you hold it in until you can't hold it in any longer. You also have a sense, to a degree, that you have very little to lose. I'm not the only one who lost his temper and struck out. Lots more handled it other ways. You had to get your satisfaction. You just had to do it your own way. I didn't see it happen very often, but it happened.

I did see one Englishman pop another Englishman on one occasion. That wasn't good, and we all hated whenever such things even came close to happening. It was one thing to strike back at the Germans and another thing to take it out on your colleagues, your countrymen. Such things happen because of the circumstances. You need to get back at something, anything. It's like fireworks. If you light the fuse, it's going to blow, but some pieces might have a longer fuse than others. You don't care much about danger because you just have to let fly. I wouldn't do that now, never had before, but I did then, under those circumstances. I don't regard it as being a big shot. I don't feel that way.

You live with yourself as a prisoner knowing that, in a funny way, you're taking care of yourself against injustice. I hate injustice. I hate it against anyone, even against my enemy. You see those cases when someone's treated badly, unfairly. If he hasn't done anything wrong and someone senior shouts him down, you get angry. You feel bad about it and want to run over and say, "No! you're wrong. He didn't do it. Leave him alone!" That's the way it is.

Work Duties, and Another Fight

Most of the time, contrary to the Geneva Convention, we were sent to Herman Goering Steelworks. We weren't supposed to be involved in anything which helped the war campaign. Nor were we supposed to be in any place which might be bombed. That didn't stop them, though. They couldn't care less about the Geneva Convention. I worked one job after another in the Steelworks. We didn't do any real work, though. We messed everything up, deliberately, every chance we got. We always threw things in the steel mixture to try to screw it up.

One of our guards was Polish, a civilian. I still don't really know how things were supposed to work there, why they had Polish civilians as guards. The Germans had taken lots of countries over and had used the people of those countries as their servants, their slaves, actually. The men who had skills were expected to use those skills. "Any carpenters?" they'd ask. "I am," someone would say. "So come forward. Show me." You'd show them, and you'd get a yellow band. You'd become a *vorarbeiter* and the guards wouldn't be able to do anything about it. They'd just guard you while you're doing the work. When you went on a job for the Germans, they told you what you were going to do.

So we had this Polish bloke. He wore an armband, and we could tell he wasn't German. He was a swine. He'd probably had never had power in his life before this experience. He probably had worked as a steelworker back home in Warsaw. He wasn't used to giving orders, but suddenly here he was, a foreman. He became authority: "Do this, and do it good," that type of guy. We kept trying to mess things up, and he would occasionally catch us at it. It was always hot in the factory, very hot. That didn't help. None of us liked the guy. I knew nothing about him, and nobody else did either. He knew we didn't like him, but he didn't care. He'd just smile. He taunted us, really.

We had one fellow British prisoner who really didn't belong in that camp. He didn't even belong in the war, to tell the truth. I don't know how he got there. He was about forty years old and the rest of us were all twenty or twenty-two. What was he doing there? He was too old to be in the bloody army. But he was there. And, unfortunately, he wasn't very bright. In fact he was really pretty bad off in his head. And this Polish foreman was always on him. The poor prisoner just didn't understand what he was supposed to do, and the foreman kept pushing him, riding him, criticizing him, ridiculing him. He was wicked. I knew he was out of line, and so did the others. There was no way that he should treat that prisoner the way he did.

To me, this foreman was having a go at this slightly daft prisoner instead of having a go at me or any of the others. He thought the older fellow was soft soap. And one time he just went too far on the wrong day. I don't know what was wrong with me, but I wasn't happy. We were in this ditch shoveling up hot cinder. We were miserable standing in that heat. It was very hot on our feet, especially. And this older guy—he had a beard, so he looked even older—he was not doing well. He was moving at about half speed, obviously hurting. This Pole started hitting him in the ribs with the stick he always carried. Over and over. And finally he did it once too often. I had to act. I really couldn't stand it.

Maybe it was because I'd been a corporal that I felt a bit different from others. When he poked him one extra time, I shouted out at the foreman, in English, calling him a "f***ing square-headed bastard." He knew what I meant. Everyone knew that word. I said, "You're good at that!"—as he waved the stick at me, "but what else? You wanna have a go at me?" And I made gestures so he'd be sure to get the point. He just laughed, that taunting kind of laugh. But I could tell I was getting to him.

I was far gone by then. I knew he would try to hurt me, but I didn't really know what he could do. I was gone. He became angry. I thought, What the hell, I'm ready. I said, "You wanna box?" Box. Same in any language. He looked at me and said, "Box? Box?" And I jumped up from the pit and he yelled, "Guards!" He didn't want to know what would happen. So I won, and I knew I'd won. I said, in a stupid way, "You no box? Tonight, you/me, box." He laughed, must have thought I was crazy. In fact, I was a bit crazy.

He didn't come back the next day, and I never saw him around there again. I did see him on the compound once, but from a distance. He'd been replaced. So I was a hero among my mates. I knew I wasn't really, though, just more stupid than the others. We were all glad to be rid of him, though, that's for sure. But there was nothing heroic in what I did. I just don't like injustice... I was angry because this man was taking advantage of another man, and I just couldn't stand it any longer. He shouldn't be allowed to get away with it. I might have felt differently if he'd had a rifle, but he didn't. I wanted him to know that he couldn't mess around with us like maybe he did with the other poor sods.

Various Incidents, including Bombs

One of the Belgians I worked with was quite friendly, and he desperately wanted to learn English, so we talked whenever we had a chance. I could learn a bit about what was happening in the war and he could learn a little English. The Belgians had good quarters with much better food than we had, so one time I talked him into letting me return to his quarters with him, and he found a buddy who was willing to take my place and return to our hut with my group.

We all walked in together as a bunch. I pulled my hat down and we talked as we walked so the guards wouldn't notice us. And the Belgian, of course, didn't have any problem getting into our compound. He was just another number. The guards just counted us, and since the numbers totaled up, he didn't care who we were. This bloke spent the night there inside our hut, and he said later he was glad to get out of there the next day. I didn't blame him.

His place was really comfortable. I couldn't believe it. Good beds with covers and chairs and changes of clothes, photos on the walls. Decent latrines. Amazing. And good food. We all talked a lot, mostly in English, and we had a good time together. The next day, we traded back, but I was able to smuggle out some of the extra food for my mates back in our hut.

One of our guards was quite elderly for a soldier—in fact, he'd served in the First World War—and he always seemed very miserable.

I couldn't blame him. Germany should have let him retire years ago, but it seems nobody was retiring in Germany at that time. They had sent the young men to the front, so they needed anyone they could find for duty like this.

He had been one of our guards for some time and was not happy with us British, and he showed it. He was a little pushy with his hands, and of course we all used to play games with his discipline and his organization. In a word, we took the mickey from him whenever possible.

Then he disappeared from our camp. We never wondered why— glad to be short of the gentleman—but on one occasion, I bumped into him when I was at work making concrete, and I greeted him, but that was about all. He stopped me to tell me how he'd been a good guard to us. He went on and on. I couldn't believe he was saying this. To me, especially. Why to me? I didn't answer. I don't think I had the right answer for him anyway.

He could speak a little English and he said that somebody in our squad had complained about his attitude to the authorities. To be honest, I thought he'd gone balmy. But he told me he'd been taken off that duty. I couldn't understand why the authorities would have cared whatever one of the prisoners said about him. It seemed to have hurt his feelings. I should have recognized that the war was nearly over, that they were really on their last legs.

I just said to him, "I know nothing of a complaint."

He shook his head from side to side, and as he walked away and tapped his nose, he said, "You remember that day when you had a French soldier take your place in the march back to prison camp? While you and the French and Belgians made a fuss of you in there?"

My mouth dropped open. I had no idea he'd even noticed it. He walked away, and I asked another guard if I could give the old guy a cigarette. He nodded and I caught up with him a few yards on and he showed me just the hint of a smile.

"Not so hard, am I? You didn't think I spotted it, did you? Not so weary as you think."

We smoked and exchanged a handshake. So there was another moment of humanity in the middle of this mess.

I still can't believe any prisoner would complain about a guard. I'd have thought it would almost be suicide. In fact, the Germans would strap you down for such a thing. But who knows? Sometimes life surprises us.

In spite of anything else that might occur, food was always the main issue in the camp. Everything revolved around food and, consequently, men sometimes became unreasonable because of their hunger. One time, a prisoner named Peter, a Brit, reached across the table to grab a loaf of bread before Blake, the cook, was ready to distribute it. Blake was in the process of trying to slice it up evenly and pass it out, and he took a swipe at Peter with the knife. He cut Peter's hand pretty deeply, and of course this led to all sorts of verbal slurs. If Peter had wanted to pursue this after the war, he could have. He hadn't really been pushy or out of line, just a bit hungry, I suppose. Blake overreacted, frankly, and took a swing without thinking.

I was standing there waiting for my share of the bread and saw the whole thing. Peter was hurt. I said to him later, "What do you want to do?" He said, "Let it go. I'll deal with it in my own way." Peter didn't really want anything done, didn't want it pursued at all. Whether any legal action, or any court martial, could have happened after the war, I honestly don't know. But the incident showed us all how touchy the food issue could get. Peter could easily have lost a finger or two in the exchange.

Thousands of men lived in these prison camps, so there must have been lots of atrocities, many of which were much worse than anything I saw. I never heard of anything happening after the war, though, in terms of retribution. Nothing. The fellow in North Africa got it later, of course, as I said. He was killed for being a traitor. But that's different. The day-to-day squabbles and disputes just seemed better left in the camp. Nothing good could come of them, and the circumstances of the camp life were such that people weren't really themselves. And especially you didn't want the Germans to know you were upset with a fellow prisoner. You wanted them to see you as a unit, as strong and together and caring about one another. You just wanted to show them that they didn't have you. That was the main thing. Don't give them the satisfaction of thinking they were getting to you.

Prisoners of war were from all walks of life. You didn't have to be a commissioned officer to be intelligent. If you were career-minded, you could do well. My own thinking at the time was that the Germans wanted to take our country, and I wanted to do whatever I could to stop them, even if I had to do it as a prisoner-of-war. I wasn't interested in how many stripes any of my fellow prisoners did or didn't have. That was immaterial. Everyone couldn't go through the war as a private. Someone had to be a leader. But for me, I wanted to go in and get it over with and get out. I didn't want to stay. I'd liked to have made sergeant. If I hadn't been a prisoner, I think I'd have made it.

During my second year at the prison camp in Germany, around 1944-45, the Allies' planes were passing over our heads by the hundreds. If it happened in daylight and we were outside, sirens would start blaring and we'd always be ordered by the guards to get into our huts immediately. They were not happy, and we didn't argue.

Most of the bombs in our vicinity were being dropped not far away at places like Magdeburg, Helmstedt, and Brunswick. We were fortunate that our compound wasn't a target, although a French camp did, sadly, receive a direct hit on one of the raids. Some twenty-one French prisoners were killed in that bombardment.

At that time the Commonwealth had better night-compass equipment than the Americans, so the Americans would fly over during the day and the British at night. They both dropped bombs near us. I saw that many times. Accidentally, of course. The problem was if you were part of an air crew, you were trained to drop bombs. What did you hit? Let's suppose you're told to go to Brunswick. We were ten miles outside of Brunswick. What is that to an airplane? From Brunswick to where our camp was located was all heavily industrialized, so we were nestled among huge plants. We were actually in an illegal position according to the Geneva Convention, but the Germans didn't care. We were lucky to have survived the attacks.

It was unbelievable to see the number of American bombers when they came over. How could so many go up? They completely filled the sky. I saw some shot down, but not many. Of course, the Germans never wanted us to watch. They made us go into our huts and they'd shut us in, but sometimes we'd get a glimpse of the planes before we got to the huts, and usually we could see them through the few small windows in the hut. When the planes came over, can you imagine the noise? I'm told there were over a thousand bombers that came over every twenty-four hours. They were just too much for the Germans. Sure the Germans might knock a plane down now and then, but that was nothing. One or two out of a thousand.

One day we were marching to another place to do some more of their filthy digging, and we approached a small railway crossing just as the sirens started. We had no place to go. The guards ordered us to sit down and be silent, and of course it upset them for us Allies to see the wild panic nearby. The railway keeper was in his uniform and he was angry with the guards. Most of us knew enough German by then to hear him curse us: "They should be shot," etc., etc. The guards tried to ease his anger and get him to shut up, but it wasn't working. One of our fellows became very angry, and probably he was fed up with living anyway; and he muttered some curses back at the railway man. Suddenly, the German threw himself at our man and smashed him in the face with his fists, just beat on him like he wanted to kill him. Two or three of us got up right away to help the chap, and the railway man drew a revolver on us. The guards jumped on the man and arrested him. The guards immediately got the police, but the police weren't happy with us either. We were finally ordered to turn around and head back to the camp.

Another day while we were in the foundry, the heat was terrible. We were cleaning out an oven and the cinders were still hot around our feet. We coughed to gain attention, but that didn't help. Then the sirens went on in there. Everyone disappeared fast, and soldiers came in and got us. We were herded down the steep stairs and into one of the large rooms with a small light like a candle. I still don't know today who else was in there, but one or two German overseers weren't happy that we were down there. I can't argue with that, but the guards with us were not too friendly, just told us to stop talking.

One or two bombs had landed near the factory, so people were quite scared. They scuttled us into another floor of the building. I knew there were women and older girls on that floor, prisoners like us but treated worse than animals, and I intentionally headed in their direction. I ended up standing near a girl who was about eighteen, and I gathered as best I could she was Russian. She was filthy, but pretty in a sad way. She pulled my sleeve and tried to hide her face. Yet she smiled and I glimpsed what seemed like a silver tooth. She made a hand gesture which suggested to me that what she really wanted was soap. She was quickly pulled away, though, by one of those creatures who was supposed to be a woman guard.

Later that afternoon I saw her again, carrying heavy bags, and she smiled and I wiped my face and nodded. She guessed, I think.

For a long time after that I carried a bar of soap which I'd received from home to give to her if it might ever be possible; soon, I'd hoped. I wish I could tell more of her, could say we met up with each other here and there and shared some intimate times; but the female prisoners were well guarded, even more than men. During another air raid, though, a couple weeks later, I sought her out again. We weren't able to have a conversation, of course, but I managed to pass the soap to her and we touched hands. That was a significant experience for me, one touch I'll never forget. I hope she made it home and remembers our touch now and again when she washes her hands and talks to her grandchildren. So be it. That was a nice day.

News of the War

After a while, we learned that the Allies were in Europe. Some of the

German guards had become fairly friendly and they'd let some news slip. I think they wanted us to see them as nice guys in case they ever got overrun. We had a pretty decent guard assigned to march us to our work assignments. I used to talk to him whenever I could, try to get him going in a conversation. It was as much to try to learn German as it was to get any information. He told us what he could, seemed to get pretty candid. One time he said he knew Germany was finished, had no chance in this war. He didn't like the war, that was obvious. He was a real person, told us about his wife and child, about his parents. Other guards loosened up a bit as the months went on also, told us things about their lives, about the war.

Around the time we began to think we might get out of this all right, everything changed. Suddenly we had new prisoners, the cream of the advance troops, prisoners who were aware of things outside the camp. They had it all. We prisoners of war were overjoyed to meet new faces, yet we were still sorry that they were prisoners. Seeing them we could see ourselves—confused, angry, frustrated. One day from fighting, winning the war. We were able to scratch every detail from them. You could never get enough. The weather? These guys had been in England just the week before. What was it like? It was a form of food for us, a hunger satisfied in finding out. We knew these guys got caught, so the Allies must be on their way. The Germans had told us they had troops in England. The new prisoners let us know they'd been lying to us about that. These men gave us new hope. The knowledge gave us hope. Then we started to think about escape.

Rumours. Remember, prisoners of war live on rumours. Lots of rumours were going around about new prisoners of war coming in. Naturally this news excited us since new prisoners meant new information. We could find out what's going on with the war. We didn't know when they'd arrive, of course, or even if they'd arrive. But one day—a Sunday, we didn't go to work that day—we heard some sort of commotion going on outside the barbed wire. We could make out some men with red berets, and I hadn't seen red berets before. They represented a force that was formed after I was taken prisoner, I think. It turned out that these were British paratroopers all part of a paratroops regiment. I'd known nothing about that, but I'd have loved to have been a part of it.

They'd just made a huge raid on Arnhem in Holland, and hundreds of them had been captured. Suddenly we saw this mass of German soldiers with more prisoners than we could count, and the prisoners all wore those red berets. Many of them were wounded and couldn't walk properly. They'd just been marched in from Holland, a long haul, a couple hundred miles. And they had recently been in England, which we learned very soon. The ones which weren't wounded all looked very healthy, not skinny like we were. They represented the top lads, fresh in the service, fresh from their training. For several of them, this raid on Arnhem had been their first action. Clearly they didn't like being prisoners, weren't used to it. They'd been captured right after getting sent out. They'd had it all, top to bottom, in one day.

They were tough guys, but many were badly injured. I stood out there watching them and could tell they were bewildered and confused, but they weren't scared. At least they didn't show any fear. They were well trained, but they couldn't grasp that they'd been captured and had to listen to some bloody German giving them orders.

I thought, *Bloody hell, if we can get one of these men into our hut, we'll find out what's going on outside.* That would mean a lot. We were all desperate to find out about the war, and about home.

I caught the eye of one bloke whom I liked the look of. I had some sense of how this would work, so I pointed to him and told the British NCO that I used to know this guy back in England. I also told him we had room for one more man in our hut. The NCO said, "Fine, then, so he's with you." He was glad to have that decision made. So I signaled to the prisoner that he'd be coming with us, and he just looked around and shrugged his shoulders and said, "Well, whatever." Then he limped over to our group. He had been wounded in the leg, even had a crude cane to help him. We took him into our hut and took care of him as best we could. We fed him and gave him a lower bunk to lie down on, tried to make him comfortable not only with us but also with his new surroundings, his new "home." Later we sat with him to talk about things. We didn't want to rush him.

When he got used to us and we got used to him, he relaxed a bit, and we asked him about the situation outside. Of course, at first he didn't want to tell anyone. That was from his training. He didn't really know us. Also he didn't know about being a prisoner, what to expect, who to trust, how the game was played. We talked to him awhile longer, though, and he finally felt more and more comfortable. He told us about the invasion at Arnhem and how they'd been betrayed by someone named Quisling—that's where the expression came from, that someone is a "quisling," a traitor—and Quisling apparently had told the Germans about the raid. The Germans had set up an ambush for the Allies, shot some of them right out of the air as they dropped from the planes. Nearly all the paratroopers were either killed or captured.

This bloke's name was Roy, and I got to know him and found that he really was from near my place back home. We talked and talked and got to be close friends. Still are, in fact. It's fifty-five years now, that friendship. He told me that in the midst of the chaos, when they first arrived at our camp, another prisoner spoke to him and said, "Stick with Charlie. He's a real character in this camp." Roy said to me, "They know about you." Well, that's nice, or perhaps not. It doesn't matter much. I did what I could, whatever I had to do to keep sane, and lots of other guys took much greater chances out there. It keeps you living. Any risk keeps the blood circulating.

When I saw the American prisoners coming through, I realized they'd had it much worse than I had. When I saw them they'd been walking for days. And when the worst-off ones came into our camp one cold miserable stinking night, I was truly stunned by their condition. We'd heard they'd be coming, but we certainly weren't prepared for what shape they were in. I remember that the gates were open and some of them had to be carried in to the compound. Terrible.

Illness in the Camp

In our camp, several men became ill during my stay there. But we didn't know what happened outside our close area, so I don't know how they were treated. I'm sure people got sick, very sick. But this was a vast camp, very large. Somewhere they had medical facilities, but I don't know where. Maybe in the town. I never had occasion to go. I know of prisoners who were taken from our camp and never came back. Not to say I think they were killed. I don't. They were taken away because they were too ill to stay in the camp and the Germans had to do something. What happened to the men after their treatment, I don't know.

I do know of one chap in the hut I was in, a man who, in my opinion, would never let the Germans get the better of him. He was from the east end of London, cockney. One of those people who can make you laugh. Quick wit. He'd been a bookmaker. He'd led a good life and was quite well to do. He'd tell us stories of gambling, of betting. That was his life. He had one child, a son, and he adored this child. This was his boy, and he loved to talk about him. But one day he just chose to stay in his bunk, never got up, never left the hut. He wouldn't go out to work, wouldn't go out for anything. He always, always stayed in his bunk—I never understood it because he got away with it. I'd try to get him going, but I couldn't do anything. He'd lie in his bunk, sick and weak, yet he'd always be cheerful when we got back. He had no more food than the rest of us, but he was always cheerful.

He was a weird source of inspiration to the rest of us. We used to ask him to say something, especially on a Sunday, when we thought about religion, and he'd lie there and tell a story. It was a way out of thinking of food. He had the gift. Nobody would stop him. If you dared to speak, you might stop him. He had this technique—probably from being a con man—and he'd tell us stories, wonderful stories, and keep us listening as long as he'd go on.

He kept himself alive by telling the stories and concealing what he was feeling, and he never got up except to go to the toilet. None of us could encourage him to get out of bed. He'd lie in that damn lice-ridden bloody bed all the time. And I used to think, He won't make it unless he gets up. Occasionally I'd talk to him about this. I remember once I was suffering with an armful of boils, a cause for concern, and I was in some agony. Nothing could make me go out. They could shoot me. That was my attitude. So I was in the hut with him alone, and I told him, "You've really got to get out of bed. You talk of your boy, a fine boy, someone to get home for. So get up." It was hard for me to understand that attitude. He didn't seem depressed and maybe he wasn't, but nobody who's starving and staying in bed is doing himself any favors. After some time, he just died. It was very sad.

At one point the Germans found a medical officer from a British Medical Regiment who was now a prisoner. This unfortunate man was brought into the compound and given part of an almost empty hut to live in. He was to deal with all the colds, flu, cuts and bruises, and any minor infections that would stop us from going out to work. And of course this would help the Germans to do other things. They supplied him with bandages and lineament and, as far as I could see, very little else. He was, of course, an officer; therefore he was the senior prisoner among us although he was far busier every day dealing with a small queue of men seeking relief and cures, like this medic was special as a magician and angel. The problem was that he just didn't have enough medicine and morphine to do his job well. Unfortunately we were so filled up with our own problems that we probably didn't think of his. He was alone with very little to help with except his knowledge

Malnutrition can cause boils, and it happened to me—my arm was aching at the workplace and getting worse, so I had to show the guard outside our hut. He saw it and said he intended to take me to see the Medical Officer the next morning, which he did. The Medical Officer talked to me about it and explained the treatment. He was very tired, too, but he explained to me the limits to his cures. He then put something cold on my eight red beauties and I immediately felt some relief.

He told me that in about three days he would lance the boils, if they were ripe, and he gave me some tablets and told me to take one each night. He saw me each day to check on me, and the third night I slept on the floor bandaged up in his hut. He saw me again after the queue had disappeared, and he told me it would be made better with little incisions. It might hurt a bit, he told me, but I didn't care since I was already in great pain.

He put something on the underside of my arm and smiled at me. "Let's get rid of them." I nearly went through the roof. I think he used a razor blade or small knife, and he got rid of the mess. I was glad to be rid of it, but I wasn't a happy man. Too painful.

He was relieved after the operation. He cleaned me up and bandaged me, gave me a tablet, and told me to go and rest and to see him in the morning. I thanked him and went to the hut across the parade ground. I was sore but really felt better, and I even slept better.

The next morning, after all the prisoners had been marched off to work, I got up to go across the ground to wash my face in the latrines where water flowed from a pipe. On my return, I looked across the deserted square and, on the only bench set, I saw a person, head down a little, and as I approached, I recognized him: our Medical Officer. In this empty area he was more than a soldier and doctor. He was a human being. And there he was without a fellow officer or medical person to discuss things with, truly without a friend to talk to. He was certainly a prisoner as much as any of us. Perhaps more.

As I reached him, I felt he had more to deal with than the rest of us. I wanted to sit and talk of the future for all of us. I said, "Good morning, Sir," and I offered him one of my cigarettes. He looked up at me and said, "Thank you." I sat beside him and lit his cigarette.

I told him that I felt bad at seeing him there alone and that he made me realize what an ungrateful soldier I was. I wanted to apologize for my lack of understanding. He smiled at me and shook my hand warmly. Then he said, "I'm not alone, young man. I have all of you, and a mob to do."

We talked of my pain. Most of it had gone by then and I thanked him for that. Then we talked of our lives and desires for our home and family, and we walked around the inside of the cage twice. It was a nicer day for that, I thought.

We prisoners finally managed to help him a little by making a fuss regarding more medication for him to use, and of course many of us "went sick" and he had to write notes if we couldn't work. Of course the committee was always supporting him, but finally he was returned to the Officers POW Camp, and he was never replaced. But the Germans, at that point, had become more helpful in regards to the illness problem. They knew they were in trouble.

Psychological Problems

The main trauma from being a prisoner-of-war came from being ordered around by people you hated, by your enemy. A lot of the Germans became particularly mean because they were on the thin edge of a wedge. They were still trying to think they were going to win the war, but they weren't, and they really knew this, deep down. I'm convinced of that. So it wasn't easy. Food was much scarcer in Germany than anywhere else I'd been. The war was going against them and they had little more than we had. Who can really blame them for stealing our food from Red Cross parcels?

I think we all knew this was the camp we'd finish up the war in. I always felt I'd get out. I suppose we all did. I never really thought I'd die there.

In late 1944, our camp started to experience chaos. We didn't know what to expect from one day to the next. To be sent on a march seemed in keeping with the mentality of the Germans at that time. In the midst of these rumours and this chaos, with snow and freezing temperatures biting at our bodies, the guards suddenly ordered us inside. There'd been some bombing, but that wasn't it. We didn't quite understand why they didn't want us out. We went to our huts and could hear a great deal of shouting and screaming. but we didn't know what was happening. It was dark. We looked out as best we could. We could see men everywhere with guards all around them, more prisoners. But who were they? We decided to go out and join them regardless of the orders. It turned out they were Americans out there. Hundreds of them. And they were in the worst shape of anyone I'd seen in all my years as a prisoner. Filthy, soaked to the skin, frozen, and starving. They were in terrible condition. The treatment they received was inhumanity at its worst by those who enjoyed it for no reason except that they'd lost, and they wanted some sick sort of revenge.

They were there, freezing cold and shivering. Lots of the new prisoners were air crew. The main reason they were so bad off, we found out later, is they'd been marching for weeks with barely any food. Some were half dead. We thought the reason they were brought in was that they couldn't carry on, or they'd die. I can just remember we had a kind of holding area and the worst of them were brought in and they were crying in pain. I would have cried too. Lots of us went over to them. We knew something bad was happening. Some of the guards we had didn't like what they saw either, and that was very clear. Nobody did. All of us British who could get in among them couldn't believe it. We thought we'd seen it all, but this was worse. Cold and wet and in bad shape. Some with no boots.

All us British felt these guys were our comrades. We went to our huts and got what we could. I gave a pair of socks to an American who was crying from the pain in his feet. His feet were black and frozen. He burst into tears and put his arms around me. I choked up. That's how it was.

I'd seen prisoners from other camps who came by our camp, and they were in a bad way, a very bad way. They'd been marching for a long time and they were sick and emaciated. These prisoners may have been Americans, I believe, but I couldn't really be sure of nationalities. We saw them from a distance, and many were in uniforms they wouldn't ordinarily wear. Old uniforms, civilian clothes. Anything they could get hold of. The Germans put anything on them. The prisoners needed clothes, so they'd take what they could get.

The guards weren't much better off than we were, to tell the truth. After my first year in Germany, I had the sense that the Germans were literally running away from the Allies. For some reason, though, they wouldn't let the prisoners go. They stayed and dealt with them. It would have been much easier for them to simply release all prisoners. They knew by then that they were going to lose the war. They had to know it. But of course the Hitler clan refused to let the prisoners go. They were much too bull-headed for that, too crazed. So there we were.

5

END OF THE WAR

TOWARD THE END OF THE WAR, things were getting bad in Germany. Prisoners were in the way. Hitler—we learned later—instructed his men to kill all prisoners of war, regardless of who they were. Fortunately, the officers realized that such an act was barbarous, and refused. Thousands of prisoners would have been slaughtered. The German officers denied Hitler his opportunity. They didn't take any notice of the order.

In January of 1945, at the height of winter—filthy weather—we heard rumours of an upcoming march. We didn't know the reasons for it, but we all calculated that it was a desperate act by a failing army. We heard it every day for a week. A march in the area. Why? We thought maybe it meant we were winning the war. This was true, it turned out, but we were just guessing.

When eventually we were told to leave our camp, the order came quite suddenly, although I don't think we were particularly surprised. People and supplies were moving all the time in and around the camps. However, I don't remember ever seeing the Russians moving out, or the other non-English prisoners. It just seemed to be us. I don't know why that was.

We knew something was going on. There was lots of movement, hustling and bustling outside. The Germans were running around, perhaps preparing to march. It was Panic Stations. Suddenly they told us we'd be leaving the next day. We were told to be ready to move out in the morning. No reason to give us a week's notice, of course, since it wasn't as though we had much to prepare. We had to gather what little we owned, because you treasured whatever you had. You had so little. A piece of wood, perhaps a stone, whatever.

The next morning, we waited outside. They only allowed some of us to go, for some reason. Probably it would have been just too many to handle. There were quite a lot of us who did go, though, and I was in one of the first groups. I wouldn't know just how many of us, maybe four or five hundred, something like that. We were marched out on that first day. We felt relieved and lucky just to get out of the camp. In fact, it was like an adventure for us just to leave the camp. The paratroopers who hadn't been prisoners long recognized an impending Allied attack. We could see the dust in the distance and we could hear the sounds of the tanks. They knew what it sounded like. The others of us had been away too long. But the paratroopers knew just what it sounded like. Roy said, "They're American." And I took his word for it. We assumed then that we were leaving because the Americans were coming too close.

In a way, we didn't really want to leave our camp, but we didn't have a choice. We didn't want to march anywhere. We knew we wouldn't be allowed to wait even though that seemed the most logical to us. We understood that the guards were fed up, fed up to their teeth. They knew they were losing and they were wondering what would happen to them. No question about that. But they still had to do what they were ordered to do: March the prisoners east.

It turned out that the prisoners who remained at Fallingbostal were later released by the Americans. I am still glad I got out of there when I did, though. One never knew what would happen when the Germans became crazed.

When we were on the march, I saw British "mosquitoes"—wooden fighter bombers, very light. I saw them coming so low that we could wave to the pilots. And they avoided attacking us, for obvious reasons. But all Germany was filled with people walking, walking, walking. It was hard for the pilots to avoid hitting civilians.

We walked and walked, and so did the guards. We had no food. None. I don't know what the guards had, but it must have been something. We walked for hours, and of course we weren't fit. Some were quite sick, and a few fell by the side of the road. But no one left them. They weren't shot, though. They were dragged or carried, whatever it took. A horrendous scene. It was bloody cold and we were all frozen. We had no medical care. It was a nightmare. I don't know how far we marched. We couldn't have walked far. Ten or twelve miles, maybe. Couldn't have been much more than that. We left around seven or eight o'clock in the morning and marched, or walked, or hobbled, until dusk.

We just struggled along all day. We stopped once in a while for water, or for rest. At dark, we ended up in a farm, someone's private property, with large fields. There was a house there, and two or three large barns. We all marched into this farmyard. The farmer came out and seemed to know what was going on. I don't know if he had any choice in the matter anyway, but he certainly seemed glad to help the guards stick it to the Brits. Probably some advance arrangements had been made. The barn was empty, so the entire group was herded into it. It was long and tall. We were shoved in there and could hardly stand up. The guards used their rifles to force us in. We were told to stay there. We asked for food and they said there was none. We asked for latrine arrangements and they said a certain number of men could go at a time, under guard, but we had to wait our turns. That's the way it was. Bloody awful.

An Escape

A few of us were looking for a chance to get away, and our attitude was it's now or never. We didn't know what the next day would bring.

Could only be worse. We were getting less fit every day. We thought about the stupidity of it all, of just going along with these madmen. And the guards weren't one-hundred percent fit, either, so we thought we might have a chance. But which way do we go if we did get away? We didn't know. We couldn't hear the Allies any more. We thought we'd try to get back the way we came, maybe meet up with the Allies coming our way. But we had to get away first. We watched people assembling for the latrine privileges, and the guards would let a few out, but we didn't know where they'd take them. So Roy and myself and three or four others went out as a group. The guards opened the door and let us out then shut the door after us. A couple guards walked us up to the other side of the barn and we were supposed to go there.

We went around the back of the barn and the guards stayed on their side. They didn't want to watch us going to the toilet, of course. We quickly scanned the area, looking for any sort of hiding place. Then we noticed a few large chicken cages and somebody said, "Let's get in the cage. Who'd know? We might get away with it." So we managed, three of us, to get into this chicken run. We stayed there as quietly as possible, and nobody came after us, nobody even called out. I don't know why. The guards must have asked about us, but they didn't seem to worry about where we'd gone. So suddenly we were in this run. We decided to stay there for another hour or so before we made our break. We didn't know about the time. We were cold and wet and miserable. So we lay down on the ground of this stinking place among all these chickens. Terrible. It stunk. And we just stayed there, lying in the muck.

After a short time, less than an hour, I'm sure, from nowhere, a boy, I now know him as the farmer's son, he came in. It was still dark, but it must have been early morning. He was about twelve or fourteen, and he was talking to himself as he approached us. He came around from one run to another. The chickens seemed to know him. But as soon as he saw us, he ran away shouting for his father and letting everyone know where we were. So we had to get out fast. I was the first to leave. I wanted out of there anyway. I took off around the back of the chicken run and bam! I ran right into the guards. Then they caught Roy just as he was getting out of the run. They hit him on the head with a rifle butt. I made a bit of a charge at them and pulled him away, because he was hurt bad. He always appreciated that, but it was nothing. Anyone would have done that.

So we were now prisoners again. Not much else we could do. I wasn't going anywhere anyway. We had to do our best. Roy ended up with a bit of a cut on his head, pretty bad, but not life-threatening. The guards shoved us back in with the other prisoners. The guards, obviously, were angry and frustrated too. We didn't get any real punishment, though. Under normal circumstances, we'd have been sent before the commanding officer for tying to get away. But not this time. This was a madhouse. All the prisoners were trying to cause problems of some sort. People were just shouting. It was mad. Our attempted escape wasn't any big thing.

We got back in the barn and soon the guards hollered, "*Aus!*" and out we all left. We just stood up and started walking again. We actually had a bit of a laugh among ourselves about our feeble and aborted attempt to get free.

So we walked on. We walked on until the end of that day, until it got dark. God only knows how far we walked. Lots of the prisoners were sick, so that kept the entire procession moving slowly. Men fell often, stumbled, couldn't keep up. What really sticks out is it was all different, not military, the way we were being treated. They didn't have the same attitude toward us that they'd had in the camps, or especially before the camp, during the train passage to Germany. I felt that if we didn't get away at that time, we'd never get away. Everyone was panicking, the Germans as well as the prisoners. The commanding officer was going crazy. Shouting and shouting and shouting. He was in a staff car, and he just drove around and shouted at people.

Another Escape

We finished up the day in this heath, open common land. And a group of us sat near a clump of trees. Roy and I and a couple others started talking, and someone said, "We're supposed to sleep here tonight, so this is the time we'd better try to get away." We all knew the time was right. The woods was only a hundred feet or so away, and we knew we could get there. None of us thought it would be hard to get away.

Although there were lots of guards, the guards were in the same boat we were in, essentially. They seemed to be as fed up with the whole affair as we were. It was nothing heroic for us to get away at this time. This was simply an opportunity to move. We had built a little fire to warm our hands, and we sat around the fire talking about getting away. The Germans didn't mind about the fire if you could find some sticks. The guards liked it, in fact, because they could then warm their hands as well. I remember this one guard named Corbuck. We'd made this little fire, and he came up to us yakking away in German. We couldn't understand him, but I thought, *This is the one. This is the guard we're getting away from.*

The other guards were nearby, but they weren't paying attention to us. They seemed to be preoccupied doing the jobs of servicemen, not guards. It was all madness. One of us, I don't recall who, just said, "Now's the time!" And I thought, *Yeah, now's the time. No good to keep saying it. Now's the time.*

A stream ran not far from this fire, just in front of the wooded area. We knew we'd have to go that way and perhaps forge the stream, maybe get wet. That seemed easy, though, even though we were already quite cold. I saw that Corbuck had set his rifle on the ground next to him, and I knew it would take some time for him to get up and load his rifle and fire it, so I felt sure we'd be out of his sight by the time he tried to shoot, if he would even bother. So we just suddenly agreed among ourselves, let's go. I don't remember which one of us said it. We all just said, "Let's do it."

I said to the guard, "We're going," and one of the other blokes shoved him down. He just sat there and looked at us, only looked, nothing else. It was like a vision. I thought, *We're not going to have any trouble with him*, and the four of us ran like mad. Fast as we could run, which wasn't really very fast in our conditions. We could hear that commanding officer shouting and firing his pistol. But we got away. It wasn't really very difficult.

Someone—most likely Corbuck—shot at us, but it was a wild shot. I still wonder if he really tried to hit us. Possibly not. It was fairly dark by then, so they probably couldn't have seen well enough to shoot us even if they'd wanted to. In fact it was black, pitch black, once we got going. We could see shades of things, trees, an occasional house, some deserted machinery, buildings. We needed to be somewhat careful where we went, of course, so we didn't trip over a log or run into a rock or step over a bluff. We were in bad shape as it was, and we didn't need another injury to slow us down.

We headed for the hills and tried to find cover. The area had huge forests, so it wasn't difficult to hide out. We were relatively certain that the guards wouldn't be coming after us anyway. How could they? They had their hands full trying to keep the rest of the prisoners from following us.

After a few hours, the sun came up. We got to a hill not far from the road we'd been walking on the day before and sat and waited, out of sight. Soon we saw some vehicles moving along the road and Roy identified them as Allied trucks and tanks, maybe a few jeeps. Then we saw the men and knew they were Allied troops, although we didn't know for sure which nationality they were. So we came running out of the hills waving our arms at them. One of the soldiers started shouting to us in French because we had berets on. The soldier who yelled at us was in an open jeep riding in front of a tank.

I shouted back at them, "You don't have to worry about us, governor, we're English." And they went balmy. They laughed and cheered and greeted us like we were long-lost cousins. It was terrific.

From what I can tell, the guards didn't look for us at all. I don't think they wanted to cause any problems with us. They didn't want us to come back and point at them for what they'd done.

This American officer in charge of the convoy told us to just follow the road back and we'd be all right. Of course he wanted to know where the Germans were and I told him they were just a few hundred yards up this road—actually it was closer to two miles. I told him there were masses of prisoners-of-war with a madman as a commanding officer. He said, "The bastard. We won't shoot him. We'll deal with him." We heard later he got shot. So that was that.

We somewhat reluctantly left the security of the Allied troops, but we went on along that road, moving westward. I don't know how to describe my feelings. We kept asking ourselves, "Are we free?" That was hard, nearly impossible, to grasp. "We're free," I said to Roy. And Roy just smiled and said, "Yes, we're free." Suddenly, after all that, there we were. "Are you sure?" I asked him. "Is it possible?"

Then one of the fellows said, "If we don't move, we won't be free for long." So we got going again, and soon a tank came and it was full of Americans. A couple men rode on top, and one of them, I remember, was black. They also spoke to us in French, made the same mistake the others had made because of our berets. We said, "Wait, we're English." They said, "Great!" And they jumped off the tank and hugged us, put their arms around us. Very nice. "You're in the right place," they said, "it's nearly over." And they gave us k-rations. We actually got food. They said, "Don't eat too much. You'll be sick."

They told us to keep going on this road and we'd see other vehicles. There are MP's coming, they told us, American MP's. "They'll put you right." Of course they were going the wrong way for us, so we had to keep moving on our own.

In another hour or so, we got back to where we'd been two nights before, the farm with the large barn with the farmer and his son, the son who had turned us in when he'd found us in the chicken run. We didn't have much pleasure in seeing the place and recalling about how we'd been turned in there by that young boy, so we just walked into the house without knocking and told the farmer we were borrowing his car. The farmer protested, of course, and tried to stop us. Tom gave him a sharp smack on the side of his face and said, "You don't have anything to say about it, you bloody sod. You were hostile the other night, and we didn't like that. You're just lucky we're in a good mood today." So we took off in his little Opal, heading on down the road. We nearly felt like civilians again. The gas tank wasn't full, though, so we knew that would cause some problem for us.

A Village
Driving along this road, we noticed a turn into the hills and could see a village nestled on the hillside. Tom Ramsey was driving, and he just swerved in that direction, hoping to find some petrol. As we approached the village, though, it wasn't petrol so much that we needed as it was a new tire. I don't know what we hit, but suddenly we felt the right front tire go flat. No spare, of course. We were just on the outskirts of the village at this time but we couldn't see any sign of life up ahead. Of course it was fairly early in the morning, before nine o'clock, so we thought maybe people were still sleeping. Didn't seem very German to us, however, to be sleeping at that time of the morning.

All of a sudden a man came striding out of a building nearby. He was a large man, tall and hefty, and he started right in speaking to us—at us, is more like it—in a rough and guttural German. We didn't understand what he was saying, but we eventually got the impression he was trying to be nice. He seemed to be in charge and, apparently, he wanted to make us welcome.

I sized up the situation and said to the others, "This bloke is scared stiff. His village hasn't been taken. He thinks we're part of the Allied force, liaison."

I turned to him, pointed at the tire, and said, "We have a puncture."

He took a look at the tire and shook his head. "*Ya, ya,*" he said. Then he went back into the building.

In just a couple minutes, three or four elderly men came out from nearby houses and greeted us graciously, almost as though we were there to liberate their village. Then they went right to work on our car. The village hadn't been overtaken by the Allies, and the villagers were most accommodating.

One of our guys said, "Hey! Check out the houses." And we looked around and saw people pulling their curtains back and looking out their windows. We later learned several of these lookers were German soldiers hiding out. We were scruffy and dirty, so I'm surprised that they had any fear of us. I was wearing a very old tunic, in fact, probably Czech or Polish, a cavalry uniform. I'd say it was made in1914 or '15, and it looked terrible. The only ones of us in their own clothes were the paratroopers who'd been captured so recently. Roy still had a good uniform. I couldn't understand how they could have mistaken us for the real thing, for the invading Allied forces, but I believe that's exactly what happened.

So these men fixed our tire and, after that, we were more confident, that's for sure. We started to recognize what was going on. We hadn't a gun among us, and of course, we didn't know who or what was in the village. We had to make the best with what we had. It looked to me that by the way we were being treated—having the tire fixed and all this politeness—we were in command. Still if we wanted to go off down the road, we wouldn't get five miles away because we hadn't got much gas. We had to play the game out. So we asked this first man, the big guy—it turned out he was the mayor, by the way—we asked for the grocery shop. And he said something like, "*Brot?*" ("Bread?"), and I said, "*Ya, ya. Brot. Brot.*" He pointed and gestured until we figured where we should go to find a bakery.

We drove the car a couple blocks in that direction and came across this bakery, just as he'd said. We could tell it was a bakery even though the windows didn't show any baked goods because it had words above the door, one of which was "brot." So we climbed out of the car and went right in. Three women were behind the counter, two older women and one younger woman. We got the feeling that they were expecting almost anything to happen, that they were frightened for their lives, poor people. They seemed willing to do what we wanted as long as we didn't harm them. Why should they think we were good people? They were just frightened. I tried to approach them in a nice way, in a low voice, gently. I asked for brot and they cursed quietly among themselves, and then they put some black bread on the counter. I think they got the shock of their lives when we tried to pay for it. Of course all we had was some old bloody camp money, wasn't worth a sou, worthless money. So we smacked it all on the counter and let them worry about it, then we thanked them and left.

We came out of the bakery and asked one of the men who had gathered around our car, it wasn't the mayor, some other bloke, if he knew where we could get some petrol. He took us get to a big truck parked nearby, siphoned some petrol from it, and put it in two big gas cans. We drove off, laughing our heads off, feeling that maybe things were really turning around. At the same time, though, we kept looking over our shoulders, concerned that someone would hit us in the bloody back. We really didn't know what was going on in that village. It seemed unreal, what happened to us.

Back on the Road

We got back on route, though, and managed to drive on that road for three or four hours. Along the way, we passed more convoys of American troops, always stopping to explain to them what little we knew. The event, that Allied movement east through Germany, was definitely a piece of history.

We continued down the road with the man's car, not going too fast, maybe only about twenty miles per hour, but we couldn't get any more gas. We kept going until the little Opal finally ran out of gas, and then we dumped it. Tom Ramsey was still driving when the car sputtered and stopped. We just left the car, pushed it into a ditch and rolled it over. We didn't really want the farmer to get it back, we were that angry at him; so we smashed it up a bit.

After we dumped the car, we started walking along the road. We didn't really know where we were or how far we were from anywhere we might want to be. The Americans had told us to stay on this road and we'd be fine, so we took their word for it. After another hour or so, we saw this big old plow horse in the middle of a field next to the road. Roy had been jockey at Epson, and he certainly knew a thing or two about horses. He said, "Let's go get it."

I said, "We can't all ride that horse, we'll kill it."

"If it's there," Roy said, "it's got to pull a cart. That's what it's for."

So we climbed over the fence, went into the field, and approached this horse. Roy walked right up to it and started talking to it like it was an old friend. Then we looked around and, sure enough, we found the cart. Tom got the horse hooked up to the cart, and Roy took over the reins, drove the horse up to the road, and we all climbed in. Damned if we didn't. Tom and I were going balmy. Some farmer started yelling, "*Amerikanisch!*" Just screaming at us. And we were laughing so hard we could barely see straight. Of course, we should have been looking for more rations, but we got too involved in this other experience. We drove that horse and cart right on up the main road where we knew there was some traffic. Whenever we'd get close to a village, we'd drive over and try to find something to eat. Most of the villages were just bare buildings and smoke, though, remains of the American offensive.

One village seemed to be pretty much intact, so we headed in and looked for another bakery. The place was deserted, or so it appeared. Probably all the villagers were hiding out in their homes. I couldn't blame them. They must have been through some horrendous times. We found a small bakery with an old woman inside, but not much was there. So we abandoned the horse and cart and headed back to the road, on foot this time, and continued west.

We passed the odd American tank, but that was about it for the next couple of hours. Finally we saw this truck with two GIs driving and we waved them down to find out where we were and what was up ahead. They said if we kept going we'd find an MP center about an hour ahead, and they assured us that the MPs would take good care of us.

They were right, and we soon got to a good-sized village where we found some Americans milling around outside a big house, a type of command center. Naturally they got quite concerned about what we were doing and who we were, and rightly so. They stopped us and questioned us. We told them we were English, and then they made us very welcome. They asked us several questions: "What's going on down the road?" "Where were you held prisoner?" We told them all about what had happened. We were filthy, but they took us into the house, fed us the best meal we'd had in years, and wanted to hear all the stories we were able to deliver.

One of the MP who seemed to be in charge said, "Take any house you want. Any house. There's nobody in any of them. The villagers have all taken off." So Tom, Roy, and I—the other two we were with went somewhere else—we went into this one big house, a nice place, and it was exactly as the people had left it. They'd walked out—or run out—of their house and had left everything behind. Everything. I felt terrible, like I was an uninvited guest in someone's private place. It was very strange. But in spite of our anger against the Germans, we couldn't do any damage to the house. These were people like we were. You could tell from the way their place looked, from their possessions and the tidiness of things.

I shall never forget Tom Ramsey while we were in that house. He snooped all around and found an umbrella. An umbrella! For some reason, he opened it up and walked around the house with it, laughing all the way. He danced around upstairs and downstairs, went into all the rooms. Crazy. He was looking for booze, a born Scotsman, and he just liked to carry that damned umbrella while he looked.

I saw Roy years after the war, and we talked about that day. He said, "Of all things, I shall never forget Tom walking around that house with that umbrella up. Whenever I want a laugh I think about that." I said, "You don't." He said, "Oh yes, I do. That moment sticks out bigger than nearly anything else during those days."

Anyway, we were in that house, and we helped ourselves to drink and to whatever else we might need later on. We didn't take anything we thought was personal, even though it was there. We would leave that to somebody else. We talked about it and agreed that things were bad enough as they were, and we didn't have to be like that. Well, there was one exception, which I can't explain. Roy, the most honest man I've met in my life, he took a photograph album. It was filled with family photographs, including photos of a serviceman, probably the son of the owner of the house. And Roy's still got it. I said at the time, "What are you doing?" He said, "I'm keeping it." I said, "That's not like you, Roy." And he said, "I don't care." He just had the needle to him. He'd lost so many dear friends. And it shows you what happens under circumstances. I've seen all the photos, and that German bloke who headed that household was just like us—wife, family, friends—but it wasn't for me to tell Roy what to do.

We all went back to the MP headquarters and slept there, among them. We wouldn't sleep in the house. We hung around that village for two or three days. The three of us went from house to house, probably went inside a dozen places, and Tom picked up an umbrella at about half the houses we visited. Strange. The MPs told us we shouldn't leave the village. They said it's still too dangerous because of the possibility of some German soldiers hiding out. They told us what information they had, and they said we should stay with them until they could arrange for us to get back to England. Apparently there was an aerodrome not far away where people were congregating. It was only a short truck drive away.

That village wasn't far from Helmir, in northwest Germany, so it was from there that we had to get out of the country. President Roosevelt died the day after we arrived in that village. The Americans, naturally, congregated around the radio all that day, and they spoke in great respect for their President, curious about the effect his death would have on the whole military situation. It was indeed a solemn moment.

Flying Home

Another day or so later, a couple of the MPs took us in a truck to the aerodrome, and they escorted us to the American authorities there. We found hundreds of other former prisoners of war at this aerodrome, and we just joined right in with them. It was an amazing experience. This was the bloody end of the Second World War in Europe, and pandemonium reigned. People were all going in different directions, talking, laughing, eating, drinking. I shall never forget that time.

We were all mostly concerned about getting home, of course. The MPs at the aerodrome told us to queue up, so we did, and we soon got to the desk where an American officer was taking names and numbers. We gave him what he wanted and he told us to form up over on this airfield and we would be called onto an airplane soon, either today or tomorrow or the next day. He promised us an airplane would be coming. Pandemonium.

One of the chaps I met there named Martin Bell—I knew him from the prison camp—decided he wanted to go out to a nearby prison camp where he'd been held for a couple years. He said there was lots of booze there and he knew where it was. We told him he might miss his plane, but he didn't seem to care. He wanted to go for it. No one knew when the planes would arrive, so he thought he might as well risk it. He asked me to hold his stuff, just things he'd collected while he was a prisoner, things he valued. I didn't know what was in his collection, but, for some reason, I agreed. He'd tied it all in an old piece of sack with some string and that was it. I held on to it all, just sat there with it, and waited. He didn't come back all that day, or the next. Finally an airplane arrived and all our names were called out, including Martin's and my own. But I didn't go. I couldn't. I had his stuff, and I knew what my stuff, worthless as it was, meant to me. So I wouldn't go. He wanted to take this stuff home, so I didn't get on.

I said good-bye to my friends, Roy and Tom and others, and they left. I sat and waited for Martin for another day, and he still didn't come back. I realized it wasn't going to be long before another airplane came in, so I got in a group that was designated to get on the next one. I decided I could take a chance and try to find Martin, so I asked one of the chaps if he'd look after this stuff, and he said he would as long as he could. I went looking and never did find him. And when I got back, all the stuff was gone, his and mine. I can't accuse anyone. Just gone. All this stuff you keep through the camps. Gone. Martin's and mine. I cursed Martin over and over. I never saw him again. He probably still thinks I took his stuff, but by that time I didn't care. I just wanted to get home.

A plane showed up and I got on. It had a mixed crew: Americans and Englishmen and one Belgian. Two or three air crew on the plane being given a lift to England. So there we were, probably twenty of us, just sitting on the floor on either side, heading home. Heading home! It was hard for us to accept. We left in the early evening, probably around six or so. It was hell up in the air, though, a really rocky trip. I think one or two of the crew had had a few drinks. Who could blame them?

It was a rough and bumpy journey in the plane, though, and we were all a bit apprehensive about whether or not we'd actually even make it. Wouldn't that have been a cruel joke, to have crashed on our final leg. It was a very ordinary airplane, and nobody seemed to know who was even flying the damned thing. They all seemed to be having a good time, though.

We flew over Belgium and of course across the English Channel. It was black outside the plane. No lights anywhere. We came across some flashes of gunfire, but I didn't know who was shooting at us, or why. It didn't make sense. We later learned that the Germans had fired at us while we flew because all of Germany hadn't surrendered. It was still going on for some. Perhaps those gunners didn't even know the war was over.

When the flight crew announced that we were over England, we all cheered like England had just won the World Cup. It got a bit raucous, in fact. Such a feeling. Incredible. We landed at an RAF aerodrome called Wing, in one of the outer suburbs of London. I actually arrived home before the surrender. Later I even got to march in the parade in England.

When we landed it was unbelievable. Absolutely unbelievable. One week earlier I'd been a filthy prisoner-of-war, a nothing. That's how they regarded us. As a nothing. And suddenly here I was in my own country, here I was at home. The reception we received as we came off the aircraft was enough to make us very proud of what we were. I'm sure everyone coming off that plane felt that pride. Even those who couldn't speak English.

6

BACK IN ENGLAND

W**E WERE TREATED AS THOUGH WE WERE LONG-LOST BROTHERS.** RAF
staff flooded the ground. They were just wonderful. I should think the
whole camp, the whole regiment were there to greet us, including the
RAF ladies. We tromped down the steps of the airplane and we were
filthy, disgusting; but a man or a woman stood right at the end of the
stairway to assist each one of us. I don't know how they did it, how
they organized such a reception. It was amazing. Everyone got the
same treatment. We were escorted into a large hangar with lights
everywhere, with flags and carpets and long tables. And as we trudged
through the door, everyone in the hangar stood and applauded us, as
though we were heroes.

It didn't matter who you were when you got off that plane, you were
treated well. They separated us, though, by nationality. Myself and
other British were sent to a room where we were de-loused. We had
to strip down, of course. All properly done. We were so very dirty.
Nasty. Horrible. And they cleaned us with a strong detergent. We
weren't given our clothes back. Who'd want them? Instead, we were
given clean new underwear and told we'd have a hot bath or shower.

I remember that bath, and I was never so happy to see one in all my life. We all had some good laughs and jokes about the baths, of course.

They didn't cut our hair, but we did it to ourselves, took turns with scissors on each other. They told us we would get proper haircuts later. We'd be seen to properly the next day. They then took us to a kind of store with a large counter, and the chap on the other side asked me was I Army or Navy? I said Army and he just looked me up and down. Obviously used to this. Probably a tailor in his civilian life. Then he issued me a uniform, which I was glad to put on, and I moved on to a place where they issued boots.

They told us we'd get whatever else we needed the next day. We were tired, but who cared? They then took us as a group back to those long tables where lots of men were already seated waiting to be served. And everyone had someone behind their chair to help. Everyone. Unbelievable. I sat down and everything was there—knives and forks and spoons and crackers and everything. They served us a good meal, chicken and potatoes and lots of bread. No alcohol, though, except a glass of beer. And I had a lady helping me and she just couldn't do enough for me. We were all treated that way. I think we were a bit lost. It was lovely even though we were tired.

It was hard to see yourself as free. You couldn't grasp it. You're on the lookout all the time just as you were as a prisoner. If someone said, "You're in England," you couldn't believe it. It was hard. You grabbed the atmosphere and tried to join in. This would only happen once in your life, so you wanted to hang on. Joy. Pure joy. We weren't allowed much food. It was wonderful to see all that, but the food was rationed to us or we couldn't have coped. Our stomachs wouldn't handle it.

They were very careful with us. Lots of doctors to watch out for us. If you had a problem, they called a doctor right now. The RAF woman responsible for me was very nice. Of course I was happy to see her and teased her as well as I could, immediately made a date with her. But we had plenty of everything. We were all alive and clean. You were afraid to close your eyes in case you woke up and it wasn't true. I can't explain the kindness, but it was amazing, and we were grateful. And we felt that this really is freedom, this truly is what we'd been fighting for, what we'd suffered for.

The military command had ordered that we should be in decent shape before we went home to see our families. That first night the officers came to our table to make announcements, to let us know about our food, and to explain what we had to do to take care of ourselves. One of the announcements was that every man in the building was to send a telegram right there and then, that night, to our loved ones. "I'll be home this week, Mother." Something like that. Short and sweet. My parents didn't even know I was in this country until they got the telegram. They didn't even know I was alive. So we were required to send a telegram just to say we were alive and would be home soon.

When we finally got to our barracks, a couple miles away in a village, we walked in and the beds were made up with white sheets and white pillow cases, and we were escorted to a bed, every one of us. Lovely beds. Like a hotel. Pajamas. Everything. I think it was around three o'clock in the morning by this time. "Have a good night," they told us, and they'd see us in the morning, but not too early. I was crying with joy and relief. None of us could believe what was happening. We had a hard time settling down. Couldn't absorb it all.

The next morning, midday, maybe, a gang of sergeants came around with tea and biscuits. A lovely feeling. Clean. Clean clothes. Wonderful. We took breakfast with ladies serving us. And an officer came in and told us what our next few days would be. Each of us eventually would be taken to the train station and would be able to go to wherever we lived. I got a pass to get to Waterloo Station. It was a short trip for me. Before that, we would go to a big room for haircutting. Again, not bad. We had to go back to an assembly room to listen to a talk about our health. And about our families not having to see us that way. They wanted the families to see us healthy. We had four or five days there and they looked after us. Good food, some simple exercise.

We had counselors available in case we needed help. We could use them if we wanted. Some of the married guys had problems, too long away. Or mother and father problems. Deaths. Whatever. It was all there. We were each asked if there was anything we wanted to talk about, anything at all. They asked lots of questions about where we'd been, how long we'd been here or there, what the guards were like, the food, the treatment. We were free to talk. We all talked about the parcels we never got.

If anyone had any information for Intelligence, he was taken to another room. I'm sure some people had a few things to say, but I didn't feel I had anything to add.

The confinement ended that week. They took us to a nearby village, High Wycombe, and we went out among the people. I'd connected up again with Tom and Roy, so we all went together. We had to go to the village to help us realize where we were, to help us get our bearings. We climbed into beautiful, clean RAF trucks, like minivans, about a dozen of us. Three or four sergeant-majors went along with us. We were in charge, though, and they would take us where we needed to go. If you said to a sergeant-major there was something you needed, he would get it. He wouldn't send someone else. He would do it himself. That was very nice, somewhat surprising.

I couldn't get over the fact that the people on the street were English people. It was just hard to accept. One or two lads even shouted out something in German just out of habit. Odd. I'd been away five and a half years. That's a long time. My mind was off. I remember our minivan stopping in the village, and we got out. The villagers didn't seem surprised or curious, so I'm sure they knew who we were, probably were used to such excursions. They just went about their business. Most of our blokes wanted to go to a pub, but I just wanted to go pick up a newspaper. We'd been given a few quid.

I went into a newsagent shop and just stood there looking at everything, trying to understand where I was. And suddenly I wasn't sure how to ask for a newspaper. It all seemed so strange to me, and I simply felt stupid. I just stood there, trying to remember what to say, actually practicing to myself. Of course when I got to the counter, the newsagent just looked at me like I was just another English soldier. All I had to say was, "I want a *Daily Express*," but I couldn't do anything but point.

I went from there to the pub, and the lads were all there. But they weren't shouting or laughing, like I'd expected. They each had a beer, and they were just talking quietly to one another. We each had one or two beers and left. It was very good.

The sergeant-majors then took us to a building where we met several middle-aged ladies, members of the WVS, the Women's Volunteer Society. They took our uniform jackets and sewed on whatever medals or ribbons we were entitled to while we sat around and had tea and biscuits. We weren't given any promotions, but that didn't matter. I confess I wore those ribbons with great pride.

We knew that the next day we'd be going home, and we were a bit afraid of going home. What did we look like? How would we act? Tom's parents had died before he went into the army, but he had a sister to go see. He'd always told me he'd never stay around Scotland, that he'd be going abroad. And I believed him. He was that kind of person. I was lucky to have him for a friend. He wasn't one who cultivated friends. He was a lone man. He loved his life—his booze and his women. Anyway, the next day came and we all went to the station. In some ways it was awful. I knew I'd see Roy again, but I didn't think I'd ever see Tom again. I went to Euston with him and I did not want him to go. Scotland was four hundred miles away, and I just didn't want to say good-bye. He was a fellow, but I really loved him. He wasn't one for much fuss. I looked at him and he said, "I'll see you." And I said, "Good. I hope so." That was it.

I had become more and more apprehensive about going home. I hadn't seen my mother and dad for a long while. They'd be older, of course, and I was concerned about how I'd behave and how I'd find them. I knew it was tough on them having been through the war. I wondered about it. My brothers Albert and Harry went in also, but Albert was taken off the line because he had TB, and he was sent to a hospital. He got out and joined an association to stand guard at home, for London. Harry went in just before the war ended and was sent to Africa, but thankfully he didn't see any action.

Home at Last

I finally headed back to London. They'd assigned each group of us an escort to the station. Once we got there, we were formally dismissed and caught the train. Three of us sat together. When we eventually got to Waterloo Station, we went to the Union Jack Club for a drink. Even though I was anxious to get home, I found it hard to leave these chaps.

Next thing I knew, I was on a tram route to go home, and I couldn't remember which number to take. I walked along the road trying to remember how to get home, how I'd have done it before the war. I crossed over the road and stood near a bus stop and suddenly remembered I was alone, on my own, had nobody to talk to. I desperately wanted another prisoner-of-war to hang out with. Seemed he'd be the only one who could understand me.

I got on the tram having no idea what number it was. I said "Peckham?" and the driver just looked at me and nodded. Suddenly I realized I was simply another person. I wasn't anyone special. I thought, That's it. It's up to me, now. I sat on the tram and looked around and saw bomb sites everywhere, and I thought, Who the hell am I? Who the hell am I? I thought of all that everyone else had had to put up with, people with children, old folks. They went through all this. Who the hell did I think I was? Suddenly I realized I was just another soldier, and nobody wanted to hear about me. And I didn't blame them.

As we got closer to my home, I got off the tram and I thought my legs would give way. There was my street. My very street. I approached it and didn't want to walk home. I didn't know what to do. I wanted to go home, obviously, but I didn't know how to behave to whoever was indoors. I had telephoned somebody, a neighbor I knew who had a telephone, and I'd asked her to tell my mum and dad I'm coming home. My parents didn't have a telephone, of course, so I had to do it that way so they'd be expecting me. And I walked down this street that I knew, and it was still all there. Nothing had gone. I turned in towards where my parents lived, and there were flowers in baskets and my name written across a big poster outside. That was common practice for troops coming home. Welcome home, Charlie.

A lot of people I'd forgotten about were around, and the nearer I got to my home the more of them I saw. I noticed one or two people whispering. I knew they were curious. I knocked at our door and I didn't get an answer. I knocked again and still didn't get an answer. That really surprised me. I remembered a way of getting in, though, a key with a piece of string on it inside the letter box. But I didn't want to go in without anybody there. So I really banged on the door. Still nothing. Finally I got the key and opened the door. The flat was smaller than I'd remembered. And there was my mother, standing on a chair in the lounge putting clean curtains over the window. She didn't even know I was there. She hadn't heard me.

So I had to make some noise since I didn't want her to fall. I knocked on the wall quite loudly. Finally, my mother turned around, and there I was. "Charlie!" she said, then, "...just let me hang this."

I don't think she knew what to do, to be honest. She needed a moment. So she finished what she was up to and got off the chair. She came over to me with tears in her eyes, and she put her arms around me and said, "I thought you were taller."

I said, "Well, it's like this, Mum, they kept hitting me on the head 'cause I couldn't speak German."

And that made her laugh, and her laughter made me laugh. It was wonderful. And she said, "You have to ring Dad at work. He wants to know the minute you're in." She said, "If you go to the pub at the end of the road, the publican knows your father and he's expecting you.

You can use his phone."

I said, "Let's you and me have a little sit-down and then I'll do it."

So she put the kettle on and we sat down together. She kept looking at me. She said, "You're thinner."

I said, "Well, I haven't eaten much." This is a mother, isn't it?

I'd gone in at about eight stones and come out at six-stone-seven, so I'd lost about two stones, about twenty-some pounds. Certainly not as bad as some.

We chatted about the family. I asked questions about my brothers, my sister. She told me where everyone was, how they were doing. They were all coming home to see me.

Finally I said, "Well, I'd better go ring Dad."

She said, "Hurry up. He's waiting. Go to the pub. You won't need any money at the pub."

So I went to the pub. They'd never seen me before. I never used to go to the pub. It wasn't my scene. I went in and there weren't many people there. I asked if I could use the telephone. I said I wanted to ring Mr. Mayhead. And the publican said, "You're Mr. Mayhead's son, aren't you? You're Charlie." I said, "That's right." He said, "EVERY-BODY!! THIS IS CHARLIE!" I got red as a beet. Everyone wanted to feed me booze. Everybody. I refused them as graciously as I could. I said, "All being willing, I'll try to get my dad to bring me tonight." The publican said, "You try to stop him."

I rang my father's business, and I said, "Can I speak to Arthur May-head, please?" The woman who answered said, "Are you Arthur's son?" I said, "Yes." She said, "Oh, it's wonderful. It's wonderful. Oh my god! I'll get your dad. I'll get your dad. How are you?"

She was up to here. That was the hardest of all. The hardest. My father came to the phone. "That you, Charlie?"

I said, "Yes, Dad."

"I'm coming home now!! Go to your mother and wait," he said. Now this is a man who never shows any emotion, but I could hear it in his voice.

And I said, "Okay."

So I went back to Mum and said, "I have to go for a walk." Then I asked, "What's Dad like?"

She said, "The same as ever, but he's had a bad time. The bombing. And you. He's had a bad time. He'll be so glad to see you."

So I went out for a walk. I wanted Dad to be indoors when I got back. I didn't want to deal with it by myself. I went back home and Dad was sitting in the armchair. I'd never seen anything so pitiful. Tears. I couldn't deal with it. I couldn't. He hugged me like a baby.

He said, "You're home."

I said, "Yes."

He said, "You'll never go away again." And it was all right. He was absolutely full up, full up. Worse than my mum. My mum held it better than my dad.

I said, "Don't you think it's about time you had your dinner, so I can finish it off?" I used to do that as a kid. He always had the best dinner.

He said, "I'll have it now."

I said, "I want you to have it like you used to have it so I can finish it off."

And Mum said, "You'll have to have yours now too, Charlie." So we sat down and she prepared it. Mum was good. I'd never seen that man break up in my life. Always a bloody hard man for whatever reason. That's the way he was. But that's what happened. The longer dinner went on, the easier it became. Then he wanted to show me off. I didn't know it at the time, but I do now.

He said, "Come on, we're going up to the pub." I didn't want to go. I wasn't keen on drinking. But he said, "I've waited a long time for this. I've heard some of those other sods up there talking about their sons doing this and doing that," he said, "and now it's my turn."

Mum said, "Come on, you go with your dad. He's been waiting a long while."

I said, "You're coming, Mum?"

And she said, "I'll just get ready and get my best hat."

I said, "I know you will. The one with the feathers in it."

So I went to the pub with dad, only about two hundred yards away. We went in and it was full. I couldn't imagine so many people would be there. I said to myself, This can't be for me. But it was. Dad was very popular. This was his pub, the pub where he played his darts. Lots of people were there whom I never knew. All the men called my dad Art, or Arty. Everyone wanted to buy him a beer.

He reverted to type: *Bang! Bang!* on the bar. "I want you all to meet my son. This is my son Charlie."

Someone called out, "We know who he is, you old sod. He looks just like you." Everyone clapped me on the shoulder and said how happy they were to meet me. It was wonderful. And most of the men's wives were there. And Dad was happy. Really happy. Of course I had beer. It was everywhere.

The worst thing for me was the publican, a big man, said, "I'd like to shake your hand. I've heard about you."

I said, "I've heard of you too." And I had. My father had had it out with him once. But I didn't tell him that.

He said, "That beer's not all, you know. I have this for you, too." And he handed me a jar, a very large jar. It had been on the counter for all those years and it was crammed with coins. Big glass jar. It was enormous. He said, "That's for you. People put money in there for you, every night."

I just stood there looking at it. I didn't want it. I didn't think it was right. I couldn't see any reason why I should have it. I was no different from any other soldier. I told Dad, I said, "It's not right."

"It's bloody yours," he said. "You bloody take it." And that was it.

I had to stand up there and make a speech, and of course I didn't know what to say, so all I said was I'm here and I'm very happy, and I'm glad I'm one of you.

Dad: "Ooooh, my boy." By then Mum was there and she finally got tears. It was an extremely pleasant feeling. I always get emotional when I think about it. It didn't matter that I was English or whatever.

It would have happened in an American bar, too, the same. It was a good feeling.

My dad liked his beer. He was a sheet metal worker. He always had cracks in his hands from the acid and my mum was always tending them. And because of the hours he worked, including Saturday mornings, the pub meant a lot. He'd go for two beers in the middle of the week with his mates, and that's all he'd have. Why not? There was no other life. Any other entertainment would have cost him and he couldn't afford it. He had no club to go to. That pub was it. Men could sit around and talk to each other.

Thinking Back

I think before I came home to England I was angry because of the amount of life—others' as well as my own—that had been wasted, angry that I got caught, angry more than anything at what I'd seen in Germany. It didn't always happen to me but it often happened in my sight. I saw things I didn't think were possible by human beings. Such hatred and bitterness caused by nothing but madness.

I didn't see so much of that type of heinous activity in Africa. There we were just left to exist in horrible circumstances, but we didn't receive the kind of brutality that we received in Germany. To me and many others, Africa was where a war should be fought, where the only people to get hurt would be the people involved, the soldiers and the airmen. We saw no civilians there. There were some in small numbers in a few of the cities, but that was it. So the war in the desert seemed appropriate, as appropriate as war could be. It was them vs. us, sort of as though it was a football match in a stadium. That was a good experience of what it's like to be a soldier.

Being a prisoner in North Africa, however, was definitely soul-destroying. You were in the pits, angry, absolutely angry with yourself that you allowed it to happen. It happened, usually, because of ignorance, not knowing. One day you're a free soldier and you feel good inasmuch as you're there to win and get it over with, and the next day you're a slave. Nothing else, really. You're furious that this has happened. If only you could get away and start again.

I don't know what I'd have done differently, though, to have prevented my capture. Probably very much the same. It's a situation that happens all the time to all soldiers. Situations come up when you don't expect them and you're not really prepared. I never considered the idea that I'd become a prisoner-of-war. I thought I'd either come through the battles or get killed. You don't think of being a prisoner. You do what you're doing that day, and when you reach dire straits, all you can do is to get out of it any way possible. So you can pick up where you were, where you got lost. If we'd had more knowledge on how to deal with such situations, we might not have been captured. Who knows? I've re-lived that capture a thousand times, and still I can't say I'd have behaved differently. I think it would have been useful if we'd been taught more, but I don't know how it might have helped.

No one could have told me what it would be like to have been a prisoner-of-war. No one could have really prepared me. The only thing anyone could have said would have to do with the First World War. Nobody I knew ever talked about being a prisoner-of-war before it happened. It just wasn't something we thought about. Most would have rather been shot than let that happen.

Once you become a prisoner, the first thing is you're totally confused. You were a free soldier, free, involved in beating the Germans or the Italians, and you felt good about that, felt that you were doing your part. You thought you were on the way to stopping these people from destroying Britain. And if you were involved in that, you were satisfied. That's what you were sent to do. Fight. And then suddenly, you're destroyed. The clock stops. You feel humble, angry, desolate. That's a good word for it: desolate. I thought of home and my parents, of course, and how they must worry. We didn't know what would happen to us. We were prisoners of the Germans, regardless of who was holding us. We knew that. The Germans were in charge. If you remember what has been said about the Germans, both from the World War One stories and from the news reports about this war—the atrocities, and so forth—you aren't sure you're just going to be a prisoner. If they just took you out and shot you, who would stop them? I know those things happened. I heard stories. They're rumours, of course. I can't substantiate them. But certain soldiers—prisoners—were in their way and had to be removed. I hope I'm wrong, but I don't believe I am.

I didn't hate Germans for my capture. That was part of the war, the big game. I was just shaken by the events. One minute you're a hero for your country and in no time you realize you have no say in what you're going to do. Your enemy is telling you what to do. And you had to realize you could do nothing. It's degrading. You didn't want to admit you were a prisoner. Total disaster, that's how you felt. And then you're finally taken some considerable distance to a prison camp controlled by the Germans and handled for disciplinary purposes by the Italians with German supervisors. That makes it worse. It's bad enough to be taken by the Germans, but it's worse that the Italians are over you. The Italians, in our minds as British soldiers, were no force, no problem. And to have to be under them hurt us. It was humiliating.

Of course once you're a part of prison camp, you're just like an insect on the sand. You're in the way. You're a nothing. And as a prisoner-of-war you have no idea how the war's going. What happened to the rest of the British army? Did they retreat from the desert? Are they gone? Where are the Germans? Are they in control of Africa? You start to wonder who's going to win the war. How many more prisoners have they taken? No one tells you anything. You hope to get information from other prisoners, but I seldom saw any new prisoners come into the camp in North Africa. That still seems strange to me, but maybe they figured the camp was at its capacity (it was) and they sent new prisoners to a different camp. Or they shot them. I really didn't know.

As a prisoner-of-war, as I've said many times, you live on rumours. Sometimes they were spread on purpose, I'm sure. And they were often very good things, especially when you were hungry, which was always. You'd think of food, food, food. All day long and all night long. You'd lie on the sand thinking of food and knowing there's no way you'll get any. Even if you got out of the compound, what would you do? You're in the desert. Where would you go? So you're down in the dumps. And of course, with me, I wondered if my mother and father would even be told I was alive. I knew anyone who disappeared from his unit in the desert would be reported missing, but would they also be reported as captured? I later learned from my parents that it was six months before they knew I was alive.

So it's soul-destroying, being a prisoner-of-war.

I saw the results of a few attempts at suicide. These never happened in my sight, though. One constant thing about prisoner-of-war life is offering some sort of spirit to others; no two persons are alike. Some-body always inspires others. Always. Others succumb. And who can blame them? It's easy to criticize prisoners of war, for whatever reason. But of course when a man is down, he's in a depression, whether it's a serious illness or just being fed up. You're aware of these people. In each camp you have a circle of friends that keep each other going. They cause laughter, they tell stories, they pass rumours, they inspire each other. So you get to know the fellows you're with, their strengths and their weaknesses. Everyone has weaknesses: Hunger. Fatigue. Illness. Depression. Anger. So you watch that person and kid with him, talk about other things. It helps.

I woke up one morning in my hut in Germany and the fellow next to me had a rope around his neck. It was a half-hearted attempt to kill him-self. I don't think he really knew what he was doing. This person just wanted out. Wanted out of life. Part of it was, though, that most of us felt it wouldn't be good for England, for such things to occur. It would be like letting the Germans know they'd got to us. We all hated that.

Most of the rumours were inspiring. First and foremost, without any doubt, food. That was Rumour Number One. That's my view. I was hungry. Everyone was. You thought food, food, and you wanted it badly. Sex? Forget it. Food was what you had on your mind. When you had food in you—never enough—you were more reasonable, you could talk, think. You'd have spirit. You'd say, "Let's do this" or "Let's try that." Prior to that you're hungry and anybody that's starved knows what I'm talking about. You can't push it away. When you're hungry and you know there's nothing coming that day, you just want to get past that day so you might have something the next day.

There might be rumours that the Germans are going to give you a bowl of soup or some bread. That lifts you for the time being. That's part of prison camp. You're told when you're going to get food. That's all. But to be lucky enough to get food, to know some food parcels are coming, to hear that somebody's seen a large train in the distance and it's full of food parcels—this is what gets you feeling well. This spreads all around and everyone believes it because they want to believe it even if they know damn well it's a lie. It keeps people going.

Mostly the Germans wanted to keep new prisoners out of the reach of old prisoners. They didn't want us to know anything. When Roy showed up, we hadn't seen any new prisoners for a long time. Men weren't added to our camp once we got settled. When you're a prisoner-of-war and you've been a prisoner-of-war for a long time—some had been there longer than I had—you get despondent. And when you've been there for years, you begin to think nasty things. You think maybe Britain's forgotten about you, that they could care less. It's the mind. The mind plays tricks on you.

Return to Italy

After the war, I took several trips to Italy to see the people who took care of me when I was hiding. I suppose I returned to that village six or eight times after I'd got home from Germany. These poor people in the village tried hard to help us. They were good people. They also helped with the resistance movement. They definitely helped me get away. It didn't come off, of course, but that wasn't their fault. I'll never forget the time I spent there while I was a prisoner and while I was in hiding. They didn't know what happened to me after I left them. When I got back to England, I learned enough Italian to write a letter and I wrote to the old man—the foreman on the farm where my colleagues and myself worked. He used to give us bits and pieces of information about the war. I always had told him I'd come back and I was determined to do so.

My parents said I was balmy to want to go. They didn't understand. But I couldn't help it. I saved enough money and went to Victoria Station. My dad insisted on going to the station with me. He said to me, "You sure you want to do this?" I said, "I'm going." He said, "Okay then."

I caught the train—traveled first class, in fact, for the first time in my life—at Victoria Station and went to Dover and from there to Cherbourg and from Cherbourg to Paris. In Paris, I rebooked on a sleeping car, and all the porters saluted me because I was going first-class. Finally I got on an express train going to the south of France. I had money, and I had a cabin en suite. All mine. And a waiter. I never expected anything like it. I was like a king for thirty-six hours. It was delightful. Then I took the train to Lyon and into Switzerland, then into north Italy past Lake Como and into Milan. That was the end stop of this wonderful, wonderful trip.

I'd learned a bit about Italian railways, and I wanted to use some of my Italian, so when I got to the ticket counter in Milan, I tried it out. I asked for a single ticket for Novara. He gave me the ticket. I asked him, again in Italian, how much it would be, struggling as I spoke. And he finally smiled and answered me very clearly...in English!

I said, "You spoiled my day."

"You did it very well," he said, "but I wanted to show off too."

I loved every visit to the village throughout the years until the old man died. Then I was very upset. He was a real man, a little bloke, but just wonderful. He had a lovely shaggy whiskery mustache that went over his top lip and hung down. He never cut it. And he had a head of steel gray hair. He always wore a Panama hat, and he had the most beautiful face, all kindness. He was a little tiny thing. I looked like a big fellow next to him. Well, he was just wonderful.

I arrived at the station nearest his home, the same station where I'd got on in my escape some six years earlier. And when I entered this village station, nobody I recognized was there. Of course I'd written that I'd be coming, but I figured that no one could afford the time or money to make the trip to meet me. I was disappointed, but not terribly surprised. Coming out of the doors of the station onto the town square, I stood there with my little brown suitcase, took a deep breath, and looked around. The last time I had been in this square it was full of German soldiers, full of them. And Italians. Full, full, full. Now—on this quiet Sunday morning—there was hardly anybody. And my thoughts went to the seats where I'd seen the Englishmen reading newspapers outside the station. It all came flooding back to me.

I could see a man sitting on a bench on the other side of the square, looking in my direction. My man. He'd probably never been there in his life. He was born in the village and never went anywhere. I knew that from the conversations I'd had with him at his house. His family never went. Their life was for work. They'd work all day then sit around an open fire and eat their food. Then they'd go to bed. That's what they did. They sat and talked. And here was this little man sitting there with his best suit on and his Panama.

I knew from where I stood who it was, although I really couldn't recognize him from the distance. He was just a figure in the distance. So I walked across the open square—no traffic, just open—and Guiseppe was sitting on this bench near an old car. I knew Guiseppe couldn't own a car. I was surprised he would even know how to get one. But there it was. As I approached, I was up to here, up to here, completely choked up. And I just waved at him. Wonderful. He stood up and he came forward like he was my father.

He put his arms around me and squeezed me and hung on, hung on. I was shaken up by all this, of course, filled with memories and feelings. I looked at him for a long time, and then, in my struggling Italian, I asked him how he was. He had this blooming light in his eye.

He was very pleased.

He spoke with a strong local accent, the Italian equivalent of a cockney accent. I had to think about each word he said, had to listen carefully. I had learned proper Italian from evening school back home. I'd also learned some Italian while I was in Italy, but really not very much.

Guiseppe said to me, "I hired a taxi." I don't think he'd ever hired a taxi in his life. He hadn't the money. I think someone in the village, maybe his family, had paid for it. And he had his best suit on, and I knew. He was very shy. He just said, "Carlo, I have a taxi." What he was trying to say was, "It's a lot of money." I had money in my pocket and I was planning on spending it, so I said, "Let's do it."

He said, "It's a long way," and I said, "I know, I cycled it with the bloody Germans chasing me." We had a good laugh. I said, "Let's get in the taxi and go back." He had told the taxi I might not want it and we'd walk.

So we got in the taxi and drove the nine miles to the village, talking as we went. We got to the village square where we'd all gathered some six or seven years before, and there we were. The taxi stopped and everyone in the village looked out their doors and windows. A taxi in the village? Who'd have thought? I'm talking about people who had most likely never seen a taxi before. In this village they'd have a horse and a cart, that's all. And they were all looking out. I don't think many people realized who I was because I wasn't important, just another person. Only one or two people knew me. They'd say, "You're Carlo." It was very nice.

I stood with the old man in the square and we talked. I said, "Let's walk." And we walked back to his house. Maybe two hundred yards. The emotion was heavy. We got there and of course they were all there. Mother, two daughters, and a son. The mother was in her sixties, Guiseppe's wife. The elder daughter, Natalina, was married to an Italian soldier. Another sister was only twenty-one or twenty-two. The son, also called Guiseppe, was a working man, worked with a horse and cart in the field.

I walked into the house and went to the kitchen. It was pandemonium. Flowers everywhere. They all wanted to know everything. They
kept touching me—"Are you all right?" "How did you get on?" I had
to explain over and over. When I told them I'd been caught again on
my way out of Italy, it was, "*Oh! Mama mia! Oh Carlo!*" The Italians
hated the Germans. I'm grateful to these people and will be until I die.
You learn to appreciate the common decency among human beings.

I found decency there as much as I ever had in my own country from
my childhood. It was wonderful. When I hear people say the Italians
do this or that, don't do this or don't do that, well, those people don't
know what they're talking about. All talk. Stereotypes. I'm guilty of
stereotyping others, I know, but this experience with the Italians
helped me see through such stereotypes.

I stayed there for two weeks this first time, living in Guiseppe's
house, sleeping in the same bed with the son. I had no idea this would
happen. I knew I was going to stay, but I didn't know where I was
going to stay. I had thoughts of staying at what I loosely called a guest
house, a small hotel in the area. That's what I was prepared to do. But
they wouldn't hear of it. I was to stay with them. I said I'd stay for a
few days. I knew there was no limit to my ticket. And I knew they
enjoyed having me around. They were showing me off. It was nice.
Each day was terrific. I had a few quid and was able to buy little things
they could use around the house. It was something I wanted to do.

When the Italians left the war, remember, I stayed there, in the
fields. The Germans were killing anybody, and I do mean anybody—
husbands, wives, children—anybody who was known to have helped
the English in any way. Any way. It was happening while I was there,
and I knew I couldn't stay there. It was too much of a risk. I heard
story after story about the Germans in the villages. Several of the stories I heard after I returned. They'd had it rough.

Visiting was a great pleasure for me. I really can't express what it
meant to me. I did nothing, of course, but I was speaking with them.
The children had their lives. They were old enough to go to work,

except for the mother and the daughter with the child. I wanted to wander over the territory where I'd spent my time as a prisoner, and I used to go out while Guiseppe was working. I'd go over it all. Where I'd been. I'd recall all that went on. It was such a great pleasure for me. I went to the house where I'd been a prisoner. I could look at the wall and the gate and the door and the kitchen, could look at it all, and I could say, "Up yours."

The house was still there, but no barbed wire, of course. I went there the second day. Everyone wanted to know what I'd do that day. They couldn't understand why I'd want to go back to that house. I wanted to go on my own. I'd say hello in Italian if I saw anyone. I'd whisper, "I was a prisoner here." Then I'd walk on. I got to the house and saw the gate. It was there. On the top of the stairs was my name, still there, carved out. I've taken Eve, my wife, there and I've shown it to her. I remember carving it with a little hunk of knife. Something to do back then.

When I got back, the place was used as a dormitory for the girls who came from town to be involved with the rice. One was Christina, believe it or not, that same shy girl I'd flirted with in the rice fields. She was back, but I didn't know it at first. Of course that was a silly piece of romance you invent when you're a prisoner. Guiseppe's family knew I was interested in her, though. They might have thought I was interested in one of their daughters, but it wasn't so. I liked that family far too much to allow myself to get involved with their children. I wouldn't want to hurt anyone. I remained just a friend. I just stood there, though, and stared at the prison house. No one said I couldn't go in or I had to stay in, nothing.

The girls were all out. I didn't know what was going on. Some people saw me coming out and had to say something. Then I saw someone I knew and remembered, and he remembered me. He was involved with some horses when I saw him. He was curious. "What was I doing in there?" he asked. Then he took a closer look at me. He said, "I know you," and he looked at me with that quizzical look. I let him deal with it. I didn't say anything. He finally said, "You're Carlo, aren't you?"

I said, "Yes."

He said, "Great!!" Then he asked again why I was at the house.

I said, "You'd have done it if you'd been me."

He said, "The girls from Novara are in there."

I said, "Not the same ones."

He said, "Most are." He said, "That includes Christina." And he smiled. I tried to play the innocent. He laughed.

I said, "She's not here."

He said, "Yes she is."

I said, "Don't tell her."

And he didn't, but I found her anyway. She was walking across the square while I was sitting and taking it all in. I knew her immediately. She hadn't changed. So I got up and walked along so as to intercept her and make it appear coincidental. When she saw me, she looked twice, startled. She stopped and looked right into my eyes. I'm not sure she believed what she saw. She wouldn't say anything.

"Hello, Christina," I said, using my best Italian. "Remember me? Carlo?"

We walked along and tried to talk, tried to re-connect. It was lovely. She was as shy as ever, and I teased her a bit. She said she thought my Italian was very good, and we shared some stories of those days during the war. She still wasn't married, but she had a boyfriend in Novarro and I'm sure it wouldn't be long before she'd settled down with him.

So I went back to Natalina's house and Natalina was there, the daughter who had married the soldier. She was as good as gold, my best friend apart from the old man. I asked Natalina if she knew where the Sergeant-Major lived. He was someone I'd thought a lot about and wanted to see. She said she understood he lived somewhere in Florence, only about thirty miles away. She said, "Are you going?"

I said, "If there's anyone in the village who will show me how to get there, I'll pay."

She said Mintin will do it. He was the journalist who was in the Resistance, the one who had helped us escape. When the Germans started taking liberties with the Italians, after the Italians had got out, he got more and more involved with the Resistance. She arranged for him to come by, and he talked with me. I told him I wanted to see the Sergeant-Major, and he said if I wanted to go, he'd go with me.

Mintin knew where the Sergeant-Major lived. The Sergeant-Major was a tailor. I never knew that. I didn't even know his surname. Of course, he didn't know I was coming. I would never have found him on my own. We got to a corner in downtown Florence and Mintin pointed across the street and said, "That's his shop, there. I'm not coming in. You go ahead."

I went over to the shop. A very Italian shop with high-quality stuff. The best. I looked in the window and thought, My god, this is the cream. Of course I couldn't help but think of that suit I'd left behind, back in London, and how good it had made me feel. "I'm going in," I told Mintin. What will I see? Will I see the boss? Will I see a member of the staff? Well, I saw both. The Sergeant-Major was done up very smart. Snakeskin shoes, the best clothes. I walked right in. I was done up, too, remember. I wasn't a prisoner-of-war anymore. I had a collar and tie on, and I was feeling like class.

He came up to me as though I was another customer and started to chat away—in Italian, of course—about how he's got the best suit in the world. I spoke in English. "I don't understand," I said. "I don't understand your language." And then he looked at me, very closely; had a puzzle in his eyes. I can see it now. He didn't believe what he was thinking. I said, "But I'll have a suit." I took my glasses off and looked right at him. He knew. He was gone. He was truly gone. It was good. He was a good friend, in spite of our circumstances.

He shut the bloody shop. Shut the shop, just like that. We went back to his office and he poured me a little whisky. It had a wallop. He and I sat there drinking and talking.

Finally I told him I couldn't sit there any longer and drink while I had a friend outside. He went out and got him. Mintin was sitting at a café across the street. He knew Mintin well from the war. So he brought him in and we all nearly got pissed. He wasn't short of money, that's for sure. He rang his wife and told her he was bringing home a man who was a friend of his during the war. Unfortunately, Mintin had to head home. I said, "How am I going to get back?" The Sergeant-Major said not to worry, that he'd get me back. So I stayed the night.

We took Mintin back to the Florence bus station and I was left with the Sergeant-Major. He drove me to his condominium. It had a lift inside. Very nice. His wife was a smart, attractive lady. They had one son, around twelve, at school. His wife must have known enough about me to be satisfied I was all right. We all talked awhile. Then she said I must be very tired. I said, "I am a bit." She spoke to her husband and suggested that they let me take a short nap before dinner. I was gone before hitting the pillow.

By the time I woke, they'd prepared a meal, Italian style. Wonderful. I showered, and then I ate with them. Great food. It was late by the time we finished eating, about ten, but Gino wanted to show me Florence. I discovered I didn't know him as well as I thought I knew him.

We visited restaurants with dance floors outside. It was a warm evening, very nice. He made a fuss of me, introduced me around, showed me the best places. I enjoyed it. Then we drove to what seemed to be the edge of town, and I said, "Where are we going?"

"I want you to have a good time," he said, and he pulled up to a brothel. Of course I didn't recognize it as one—it didn't have "Brothel" written over the doorway—so I was thinking he was taking me to meet a friend. He was. I don't think he actually used the brothel, but he knew everyone there. He spoke to the madam and they took a look at me. I still didn't know it was a brothel, believe me. I was so innocent. I can't describe it very well. It looked something like a house, but it was more like a factory with a long corridor. Doors were open. Women sitting around. Beautiful. They knew I wasn't Italian.

They spoke in Italian thinking I didn't understand, but I did. What they said they wanted to do with me was an education. I heard volumes. Some wasn't bad. Some was terrible. The things they were saying to each other were amazing. No way was I going to climb in the sack with one of these women.

So I came out the other end. Gino was standing there with the madam. He asked me if I had a good time. He didn't know I didn't have a woman. Then he took me back to his apartment and told his wife where he'd taken me. He thought my Italian wasn't good enough to understand what he was saying, and he told her what he thought happened. She giggled. After he told her, when he wasn't around, I said to her that I didn't have a woman. She said, "Why not?" I said I didn't want to be pissing out of five holes.

The next day, before I left, he offered me a new suit, but I didn't take it.

When we got back to the village, he went around and visited with all the people. He hadn't seen them for years. They all knew him, of course, and they liked him. I believe it meant a great deal for him to return.

I've been back several times now. One time, on one of the visits, I was talking with Natalina, whose husband had died by that time, and she asked, "Do you remember Antonio?"

I said, "Yes, he was one of the guards." He was a reluctant guard. He just didn't like it. He wanted to be a fighter. He was never happy. But he was also a man I could manipulate. Not all that bright those days, seemed fed up.

She said, "He's very ill."

"Where does he live?" I asked.

She said, "Three miles away, where he's always lived."

I asked if she thought I could go there. "Does he have a wife?"

She said, "Yes, he's married." She said I could go with her the next day. She had a bike. I used to go places with her all the time. She didn't care what people thought. So we rode out of town and finally came to a small, well-kept house. She said, "That's Tony's."

I asked if she'd go first and talk to Antonio's wife. She told me to come with her. I spoke to the lady also. I spoke enough Italian so she understood me. He was in the bedroom, so I asked if I could go in. She said, "Please do."

He was very thin. All I could see was his head. Practically nothing else. I recognized him, though. He was very close to death. We hadn't always seen eye to eye back then, during the war. I used to talk to him sometimes and tell him to put down his rifle and enjoy the day. He didn't always like that. So this time I told him who I was and how he'd know me from the war. He looked at me, just barely. I asked if he remembered. "*Si, si.*" He was glad, I think, that I'd come. I just sat there for a while, looking at him, remembering. In a few days he was gone. It was sad.

On another trip I was in the street in the village, and one of the former guards came up to me and wanted to talk. I remembered him well, and he was a real bastard during the war, treated us all rotten. So I told him to piss off. I couldn't get angry with him because he was too dumb. He was always trying to make out that because he was a guard, he was better than the rest of us. Nobody worried about him, but nobody much liked him, either. He was an idiot. I never saw him again after that incident in the street.

Epilogue:
CHANGE IN ATTTUDE

WHEN I CAME OUT OF THE ARMY, I wasn't looking for a tuppence-ha'penny job in an office. I felt I was better than that. Because of the discipline in the army, which teaches you how to act and think like a man, how to deal with other men—with all those things you become a better person. You stop feeling sorry for yourself, which is what I was doing before I went in. I figured the world owed me a living. Then the war was over. England was no better off. England was broke. I thought, I'm not standing still while the country gets it together. I knew in myself that I could make it, knew from my experience being in a prison camp and eating humble pie from the Germans. That was it. Never, never again. I got through that, I told myself, and I could by-god get through anything else this world threw at me. I thought about that a lot, actually, and it gave me a great deal of motivation.

But I planned to do it in a sensible way. I knew I'd have to work bloody hard developing my knowledge and my skill. In other words, I had to go about learning something. Not just on the job but outside the job. By that time I was twenty-six years old and I'd developed a discipline in myself and a tolerance for other people. I never again used the excuse: Well, it's not your fault. It is my fault. Whatever happens. That's a fact. I knew the only way up was to work hard. And I did, I worked hard until I was sixty-five, and some of the work was a pain in the butt. But I went home every evening satisfied with myself. I knew I could stand it. I'd been in much worse circumstances in North Africa and in Germany than anything Mother England could put me in.

Once I was working in the Covent Gardens. It wasn't the job I'd expected, but I had to make it what I wanted. There's nobody to come along and say, "Here's some money. You've been a good soldier." One time I did something I wouldn't have done before the war. When I came back to England, the country was still on rations. They give you a slip of paper and you get this or that. Everything was a struggle, but the struggle was the same for everybody. I'd worked so many hours for my job, I nearly knocked myself silly, but I knew this was a means to an end so I'd bloody well do it. And I'd believed that I could get myself higher and higher. Some of the days were bad, so bad I could have walked away from that job and never gone back. My boss used me. He wasn't a mean man, but he was a thoughtless man. He never realized what it was like being a lowly employee of his, let alone being a prisoner-of-war.

I was his first employee who'd come back from the war. The only thing he knew about me was that I'd been in the army and I'd been a prisoner-of-war. That's all you can expect. I used to come home sometimes at seven after starting at four in the morning. I liked to go out with a friend, Fred. He'd been in the navy. I used to make arrangements with Fred—Tomorrow night I'll meet you at such-and-such a time, we'll go to the cinema. If we can get a couple birds, so be it. If not, we'll have a good time anyway. We'd get together when we could. We were good friends. Trusted each other completely. I'd let him down a few times and he'd done the same with me, but not often. But going out for an evening with him was important to me.

I used to come home from work and be late to meet Fred. So I'd have to rush home and scramble through dinner, then run to the tube train and from the tube train to the bus line, and I'd already be late. This couldn't go on. Fred would end our friendship. I didn't want to be late, but I didn't feel that I could tell the boss, "Look, I can't stay tonight." I felt I had to swallow whatever he gave me and do it. I'd come home from work and dinner would be warming in the oven. I'd say, "I'll just go in and wash my hands," and I'd lie down a second and fall asleep. Mum would come in after a while and find me. She knew I was worn out. She wouldn't wake me up. And of course I'd let my friend down. So finally I told Fred I couldn't go out. It wasn't worth his while. We remained friends, but we didn't see each other any more.

One day I'd worked hard from four in the morning until midday, no stop, and the boss said, "I've had a load of potatoes that I want delivered. Pick them up over at McGrady's garage." I knew he'd probably had an arrangement of some sort. These should have been sent through the government and rationed, but he said he'd had this big shipment delivered. I knew this garage. I'd been there once or twice.

He said, "I want you to go fill the lorry up."

I said, "You want me to fill it up?"

He said, "Yes, Charlie, you can do it."

And I said, "You are kidding me, aren't you?"

He said, "I've got some fight tickets coming up soon."

I should have told him to shove his tickets, and his bloody job, up his ass. That's what I should have said.

I drove his three-ton truck to the garage some ten or twelve miles away. By then it was one o'clock. I got to the garage and it was full of potatoes. Each sack was 100-weight. I was to load the truck by myself, and it was up high, not low. So I had to pick up the sack, carry it to the truck, set it down, get on the truck, and stack it properly. All the sacks had to be stacked properly or they wouldn't ride. I put five ton of potatoes on the truck by myself, and all the time I was putting them on, I knew I wasn't doing myself any good, so I got angrier and angrier and angrier. How I did it, I don't know. How I didn't get a hernia, I don't know

I finished up at about six, and I went to his house, a bloody mansion. And he said, "Well done, Charlie, I knew you could do it."

I said, "I'm going home now to get my breakfast, my lunch, and my dinner."

And he laughed and said, "You're all right, Charlie. No one else could do it like that. And you're in line, you are."

I said, "I've never heard so much bollix in all my life." I was angry.

He didn't smile then. He said, "Come on, Charlie. Don't take it like that."

I said, "I'm absolutely whacked. I'm not fit to drive the vehicle." I lived on the other side of London. He wanted me to unload them that night to six different shops. I said, "You know what you can do, don't you. I'm through with this load."

He said, "You don't want to talk to me like that, Charlie."

I said, "I'm through."

He said, "You don't mean it."

I said, "Try me tomorrow morning. Don't come near me now." And he knew I meant it.

So I left the truck and went home by tube and bus. I got home at about nine o'clock that night and my mum said to me, "You're out of your mind."

I said, "I'll buy that, Mum, I am. I am!" And I went to the bedroom and fell on the bed and fell asleep. And my mother didn't tuck me in. She just let me sleep.

I got a call the next morning and my boss told me to go out and offload the potatoes from the back of the truck, and I just said, "You do it."

And he did. He did off-load them. I thought, Good. That's what you need to do. I'll give him his due. He did it. Of course there was nobody else. He put on some old clothes and went out and drove that truck. But he got some staff from each store to unload the truck. I didn't go to work the next day. I thought, the hell with you. You'll have to ring me.

And he did. He rang me and said he wanted to meet me the following morning. "I'll bring the truck," he said." We'll have a bit of breakfast together in Covent Garden."

I said, "I'll be there."

So I went the next morning early and he was already there, in his best brown suit. "Come on, Charlie, let's go and have a bite to eat," and he put his arm on my shoulder.

I was sore. I said, "Get your hands off." So we went in and had breakfast. He was very quiet. The place was full of market people. Lots of hard men in there. Hard. He was quiet, didn't want any problems.

I said, "How was it with the lorry?"

He said, "I see your point."

I said, "You didn't even load them on."

He said, "No I didn't." He said, "Can we forget it?"

I said, "Don't you ever, ever do that to me again." I said, "I did it because I want to get on, but I'll get on with you or without you. Don't you ever do that to me again." And that evening we went to the fights at the Royal Albert Hall, and that helped.

I think the prisoner experience helped to prepare me to get myself off Shit Street. And I never lost out on those experiences because it made me for the first time feel I was somebody. In the past, I'd used the country, I'd used England, as an excuse. But now that I'd become six years older, I could deal with life as it was.

I continued to work for him for another couple of years. I'd be at the market at four o'clock with my lorry and everybody else would be there buying what they needed, and I'd sit there with an empty truck. He'd never give me money to go and buy the goods we needed. If he had given me a hundred pounds, two hundred pounds, I could have helped him a lot. I knew the game. I could do it as well as he could. But I didn't have the money. I'd wait for him to show up in his bloody Rolls Royce. "Hi Charlie boy. Isn't this a lovely day?"

The others used to laugh at me. "See you tomorrow, Chas, you still be here?" It was like being a prisoner.

One day he went too far. He came up all greasy-like. He loved to show off. "Charlie boy? Let's go have a cup of tea." I'd been waiting for him to buy something. I didn't want a cup of tea. I wanted to go, to get on with the day. I wanted to do the business and go home. It just got to me one too many times. I really wanted a promotion to buyer, but he wouldn't give it to me.

So I walked up to him on the street and I said, "You can stick it."

"What's the matter?"

"Matter?!! Matter?!! It's ten o'clock. I've been here six bloody hours. I have an empty lorry. When am I going home?"

"It's the game, boy."

And I said, "Look around you? What do you see? Empty lorries, empty curbs. All gone. All bought. The f***ing stuff you have left is crap. They've all bought the good stuff. You're a ponce."

It didn't make me feel good, but I didn't care. It was me at my worst. I really didn't care. And he walked away shaking his head. I'll never forget that. He said, "I thought we were friends. I never thought you'd do this to me."

I went home to my mum. She said, "Don't tell me you've had an early day."

I said, "Mother, I've done nothing. And I'm doing nothing."

She said, "What do you mean?"

I said, "I've quit."

She said, "Thank the lord for that." She said, "He was killing you. All those bloody boxes."

He started ringing me up. I said, "Ring me up all you want. Just send my employment cards at the end of the week. Send me the money." I went back on a Saturday morning. My cards were there and my money was there, but he wasn't.

Effects of Prison Life

So what I think about prison life is that what I saw was worse than my being there. Hard to explain, but that's what I felt. I always thought I'd get away, I'd survive, but I wasn't sure about the others. When I finally did get out and managed to get back into British lines, I wasn't really angry. I felt contempt for the enemy, more than anything else. What they'd been doing to us was by that time happening to them. Worse, since their country was being taken away from them. The Allied troops came in and beat the Germans by winning the war. That had to hurt.

Afterwards, I didn't walk around thinking about prison life or the Germans or what they did. I was excited to be alive. It takes a while to adjust to the idea that you're free. It's hard to shake away the feeling that someone will put a hand on your shoulder at any minute. I used to have bad dreams of being a prisoner, but they're gone now.

Even today, though, if I see injustice, if someone says something to or about someone that I don't think is right, I feel that I have to speak. I don't like to see that. If I were sensible I wouldn't act that way, but for me—I don't want it but it's there—I have to act. I think that may be an effect of being a prisoner, of being so helpless in so many situations.

I've occasionally become annoyed at work when senior staff criticized me. I've wanted to say, "Hey. I've had three years in a bloody prisoner-of-war camp. What can you say to me?" But you can't do that. You can't go through life making mistakes and using your experiences as a prisoner-of-war as some sort of excuse for why it happened. You never can tell your boss you've been a prisoner-of-war. If I'd done that, if I'd used it as an excuse, that would have been wrong. That's not me. I have to deal with things as one human being to another. If you use your background, something that's happened to you, to get out of a jam, that's not good.

There are lots of ways of being disillusioned about the war. Millions were killed. Others wounded or tortured. You could be shell-shocked, or you could be land-mined, like my brother-in-law, Bobby, and lose your leg. Lots of ways men and women suffered greatly. But

I really don't go through my days thinking about being a prisoner-of-war. That's history. That's not the worst thing that can happen to you. I see it another way now. I don't harbor hatred for what was done. It's a bit of war. I'm lucky I came out alive, with all my limbs.

It probably has helped me be more tolerant, actually. Before the war, I was disgusted with England for my having a meager existence. I was going through a bad time, and I wasn't familiar with the state of the country, only with what I was doing. I wasn't doing well. My own fault. I shouldn't have let anything stop me from getting on, but I did. I used the country as an excuse for my being a poor working man with no future. That's the way I was, and I made no bones about it. I was an angry lad.

I remember the period between when I was about fourteen until I was eighteen trying to get a job that would be useful to me to advance my life to a better standard of living, but I wasn't clever enough or experienced enough to know how to go about it. In my mind I thought this was England's fault. Lots of other boys and girls my age were going nowhere, just doing a job. No futures. You could be sweeping a courtyard for ten shillings a week. There you go. Nowhere. You'd still be doing it when you became a man. It was like that.

I used to go to the west end and see people with money, see them doing things, have a car. I could never see that for me. Never. I was glad for the war because I felt it would give me the chance to go abroad, to be someone. I never had the money to go to France. That's the way I was and that's the way my friends were.

Maybe my friends weren't so out front about it as me. I was angry and ready to stand up to anybody at that time. So when the government said, "We want you," I was ready to go and relieved. I felt sorry for my mum and dad, of course, but I wanted to go. I gave up being in charge of my life when I joined up, but frankly I think I liked that. I must say I appreciated the military. It made me think better about myself. And I was with another twenty kids my same age, exactly my same age, twenty years old. All from different jobs, different housing, different experiences, but all the same. Suddenly I was in a uniform, properly dressed in a uniform, and I was a soldier. I went to bed and I woke up on schedule, and I was paid. I had money. I couldn't make excuses any more about being different from this guy or that. I couldn't use that. That was me feeling sorry for me as a civilian. But not as a soldier. I couldn't do that anymore.

They wanted to train you, make you fit, cut your hair, make you smart. It was great. They wanted volunteers. So I volunteered. Nothing brave. It was new. I was going abroad. And I learned from the army that I can't expect people to sort me out after the war and say, "That poor man, he's had no life." It's what you do with your life when somebody's taught you how to conduct yourself. I'm glad I went through the army, and of course I'm glad I came out. How I behaved as a soldier is for other people to judge.

I did as I was told and I behaved as a soldier. Not a regular soldier but a soldier for a war. Whatever was going on, I said, "Yessir." If the war hadn't come along, I don't know what I'd have been. Knowing me as I am, I don't think I'd be as well off as I finished up. I think I'd have gone abroad as a single person, just gone, and maybe even stayed there. I really thought if I couldn't make it before the war I'd have to get up and kick myself in the ass and not worry about what the government would do for me.

A Reunion

About three days after I got home, I went out to get a haircut. Dad was at work. I was sitting in the barber's chair and the barber was chatting away as though I'd always been there. And I thought, You don't know, do you? You don't know where I've just come from. It was like I'd never left London. I paid him and went home and told Mum I was going out again. I was lost. I just wanted to be among people, just wanted to go out.

When I got home, my mum said, "You've got a friend here." I had no idea who it would be. I hadn't expected anyone, certainly no one

I knew in the army. Never in a million years did I think it would be Tom. Maybe Roy, but not Tom. But there he was. I never expected him. I said, "You sodden bastard. You shouldn't do this to me."

His eyes were wet. He said, "Where's the pub?" So we walked to my dad's pub. When my dad came home a couple hours later, he ate and changed his clothes and said to my mum, "Come on. We're going out." And he came to the pub and joined us.

They knew me by then at the pub, but they didn't know Tom. When I walked in, it was all, "Oh hello, Charlie. Come on in, great to see you, have a beer."

Tom said, "I like that."

So Tom and I were sitting down there when my dad came in. My dad made quite a fuss about it. He'd heard of Tom but hadn't met him. Tom had gone home to Scotland by that time and had had a couple days with his sister in Glasgow, but then he got back on the train and came to London. Didn't even know where I lived, but he found me. That was Tom. He said there was nobody there for him, at home, nobody for him to stay for.

Next morning we got up and had breakfast and Tom said, "Let's go for a walk." I told Mum we were going out, and she said, "When are you coming home? Will Tom be with you?" I said, "Don't ask. I don't know." So we went out for a walk, and Tom right away said, "Where are they, the girls? Where are the hookers?"

I said, "The hookers?! You must be kidding."

He said, "You're not coming, are you?"

I said, "No, I'm not coming. I've heard about where they are, but..."

He said, "That's it!" So I pointed him in the right direction and he got on the next bus. Not a damn thing I could do or would do. He was going his way. He was gone, on a bus. Gone. So I went home.

Mum said, "So where's Tom? Is he enjoying himself?"

I said, "You know Tom. We might see him again or might not. He's in a pub."

Next morning he came back and we had another good breakfast. He cleaned up. Never said a word about it. We went back out to the pub. Then he said he'd better get going, should get home. I said all right. Then I asked, "How was it?"

He said, "I screwed myself silly."

He told me about his adventures. I guess he'd had three ladies. I saw him get back on the train but I never saw him again.

I got one letter from him a few years later. I didn't even know he could write. He was my man, I'm telling you. I know he didn't stay in Scotland for long. He must have roamed the world. He wouldn't have written if I hadn't written him. He went abroad. He told me he would. I think he went to Australia, but I didn't hear from him. I tried to locate him through friends. His name was George, actually, not Tom. George Ramsey. He just went by Tom. He was a good man. He was captured in Africa, about the same time I was. He looked like Sean Connery. Talked like him, too. Head full of black hair that was never combed. He had a massive carbuncle in the middle of his face, but he ignored it. I asked him about it once and he said he'd take care of it when he got home.

I went to a retreat about twenty years ago, the Queen's Parade, it was called. Big deal. Any servicemen or ex-servicemen could go. My brother-in-law Bobby and I went. We took our wives. The Queen came out. We stood there, and in front of us were the Chelsea Pensioners, all in their red uniforms. And I saw among them the old sergeant-major from Germany, from the camp. I sat there and stared at him. I kept looking at him, thinking, I know you. He had the insignia on his arm and he looked just like I remembered him.

I said, "Bobby, take a look." But Bobby was only interested in the Royal Family. Most people were. I wanted a photograph of the sergeant-major so I asked Bobby's wife to take it. I said, "I want a picture of that Chelsea pensioner down there." She said, "Which one?" I said, "That one there. Try to get the side of his face. I'm bloody sure I know him."

I thought Roy might be able to identify him from the photograph, so I sent it to him and he said, "For sure. That's the fellow. The same one from the prison camp." I couldn't believe it. He was a paratrooper. Might have only been thirty-five years old at the time. Probably ten years older than me, but I can't tell. Roy said, "I remember him from when we were fighting. Even when he was a prisoner, he was a sergeant-major prisoner." He wasn't the same as us. He was a man that you knew if you were in trouble, you'd feel better as long as he was with you. He was of that ilk. Like Tom, the kind of man I'd have loved others to have seen. If he'd been 6'10" he wouldn't have been any bigger. He was a real soldier. The army was his life.

I often think of one day shortly after I'd got out of the service. I returned home and told my mother that I was going to my bedroom to lie down. She said, "It's ready, Son." I went in, closed the door, and opened my old wardrobe. There was my suit, hanging there, smelling of camphor and slightly different from my dreams. I put the jacket on and it didn't fit. "Never mind," I said to it. "You kept me going a long time." I threw it up in the air and kissed it as it fell into my arms. "We're in the same room together now."

SUMMARY OF DATES:

JUNE 30, 1939: Conscription
SEPT. 7, 1939: England declares war on Germany
SEPT. 16, 1939: Entered the army
JAN., 1940: Sent to France
FEB., 1940: Sent to North Africa (Alexandria)
June 1942: Captured by the Germans, sent to a camp near El-Adam, outside Tobruk
Dec. 1942: Transported to Tripoli, shipped across the Mediterranean to Sicily, taken to a camp in Capua for 3-4 weeks
JAN. 1943: Transferred to a camp near Rome
MAR. 1943: Transferred to Camp #73 on west coast of Italy
APRIL 1943: Transferred to Camp #53
OCT. 1943: Transferred to Working Camp in Monticello
AUG. 1944: Italians quit the war
DEC. 1944: Attempted escape from Italy to Switzerland, re-captured
LATE DEC. 1944: Transferred to Germany through Brenner Pass (with 2-week stopover in Innsbruck)
JAN. 1945: Fallingbostal Prison Camp, Germany
APRIL 1946: Left Fallingbostal, escaped from the march
APRIL 1946: War ends in Germany
APRIL 1946: Returned home to England

Other Books by Pleasure Boat Studio: A Literary Press

The Immigrant's Table, MARY LOU SANELLI
  ISBN 1-929355-15-7, $13.95, POETRY

The Enduring Vision of Norman Mailer, BARRY H. LEEDS
  ISBN 1-929355-11-4, $18, LITERARY CRITICISM

Women in the Garden, MARY LOU SANELLI
  ISBN 1-929355-14-9, $13.95, POETRY

Pronoun Music, Richard Cohen
  ISBN1-929355-03-3, $16, SHORT STORIES

If You Were With Me Everything Would Be All Right, KEN HARVEY
  ISBN 1-929355-02-5, $16, SHORT STORIES

The 8th Day of the Week, Al Kessler
  ISBN 1-929355-00-9, $16, FICTION

Another Life, and Other Stories, EDWIN WEIHE
  ISBN 1-929355-011-7, $16, SHORT STORIES

Saying the Necessary, EDWARD HARKNESS
  ISBN 0-9651413-7-3 (HARD) $22; 0-9651413-9-X (PAPER), $14,
  POETRY

Nature Lovers, CHARLES POTTS
  ISBN 1-929355-04-1, $10, POETRY

In Memory of Hawks, & Other Stories from Alaska, IRVING WARNER
  ISBN 0-9651413-4-9, USA $15, 210 PAGES, FICTION,

The Politics of My Heart, WILLIAM SLAUGHTER
  ISBN 0-9651413-0-6 , USA $12.95, 96 PAGES, POETRY,

The Rape Poems, FRANCES DRISCOLL
  ISBN 0-9651413-1-4, USA $12.95, 88 PAGES, POETRY,

When History Enters the House: Essays from Central Europe,
  MICHAELBLUMENTHAL ISBN 0-9651413-2-2, USA $15, 248 PAGES,
  NONFICTION

Setting Out: The Education of Li-li , TUNG NIEN, TRANSLATED FROM
  THE CHINESE BY MIKE O'CONNOR, ISBN 0-9651413-3-0, USA $15,
  160 PAGES, FICTION

Our Chapbook Series:

No. 1: *The Handful of Seeds: Three and a Half Essays*, ANDREW SCHELLING ISBN 0-9651413-5-7, USA $7, 36 PAGES, NONFICTION

No. 2: *Original Sin*, MICHAEL DALEY
ISBN 0-9651413-6-5, USA $8, 36 PAGES, POETRY

No. 3: *Too Small to Hold You,* KATE REAVEY
ISBN 1-929355-05-X, $8, POETRY

No. 4: *The Light on Our Faces: A Therapy Dialogue*, LEE MIRIAM WHITMAN-RAYMOND, ISBN 1-929355-12-2, $8, 36 PAGES, POETRY

No 5: *Eye*, WILLIAM BRIDGES, ISBN 1-929355-13-0, $8, 20 PAGES, POETRY

No.6: *The Work of Maria Rainer Rilke: Selected "New Poems" in Translation,* TRANSLATED BY ALICE DERRY, ISBN 1-929355-10-6, $10, 44 PAGES, POETRY

Forthcoming Pleasure Boat Studio books:

Schilling, TERRELL GUILLORY
ISBN 1-929355-09-2, $16, FICTION

From our backlist (in limited editions):

Desire, JODY ALIESAN
ISBN 0-912887-11-7, $14, POETRY (AN EMPTY BOWL BOOK)

Dreams of the Hand, SUSAN GOLDWITZ
ISBN 0-912887-12-5, $14, POETRY (AN EMPTY BOWL BOOK)

Lineage, MARY LOU SANELLI
NO ISBN, $14 POETRY (AN EMPTY BOWL BOOK)

P'u Ming's Oxherding Tales, RED PINE
NO ISBN, $10, TRANS FROM CHINESE WITH ILLUSTRATIONS, FICTION (AN EMPTY BOWL BOOK)

The Basin: Poems from a Chinese Province, MIKE O'CONNOR
ISBN 0-912887-20-6, $10 / $20, POETRY (PAPER/ HARDBOUND) (AN EMPTY BOWL BOOK)

The Straits, MICHAEL DALEY
ISBN 0-912887-04-4, $10, POETRY (AN EMPTY BOWL BOOK)
In Our Hearts and Minds: The Northwest and Central America,
ED. MICHAEL DALEY ISBN 0-912887-18-4, $12, POETRY AND PROSE
(AN EMPTY BOWL BOOK)
The Rainshadow, MIKE O'CONNOR
NO ISBN, $16, POETRY (AN EMPTY BOWL BOOK)
Untold Stories, WILLIAM SLAUGHTER
ISBN 1-91288724-9, $10/$20, POETRY (PAPER / HARDBOUND) (AN
EMPTY BOWL BOOK)
In Blue Mountain Dusk, TIM MCNULTY
ISBN 0-9651413-8-1, $12.95, POETRY (A BROKEN MOON BOOK)

ORDERS:
Most Pleasure Boat Studio books are available directly from PBS or
through any of the following:
SPD—Tel: 800-869-7553, Fax 510-524-0852
Partners/West—Tel: 425-227-8486, Fax: 425-204-2448
Baker & Taylor—Tel: 800-775-1100, Fax: 800-775-7480
Ingram—Tel: 615-793-5000, Fax: 615-287-5429
Amazon.com
Barnesandnoble.com

for PBS orders:
Tel/Fax: 888-810-5308
Email: pleasboat@nyc.rr.com
Website: www.pbstudio.com

HOW WE GOT OUR NAME:
from Pleasure Boat Studio,
an essay written by Ouyang Xiu,
Song Dynasty poet, essayist, and scholar
(January 25, 1043)

"If one is not anxious for profit, even at the risk of danger, or is not convicted of a crime and forced to embark; rather, if one has a favorable breeze and gentle seas and is able to rest comfortably on a pillow and mat, sailing several hundred miles in a single day, then is boat travel not enjoyable? Of course, I have no time for such diversions. But since 'pleasure boat' is the designation of boats used for such pastimes, I have now adopted it as the name of my studio. Is there anything wrong with that?" -**Translated by Ronald Egan**